WILDERNESS RANGER
▲▲▲
COOKBOOK

This book was produced by the Society for Wilderness Stewardship and Osprey Packs, Inc. in cooperation with the four federal land management agencies that administer congressionally designated wilderness.

Additional cookbooks and materials are available through the Society for Wilderness Stewardship. The Society is a not-for-profit 501(c)(3) and the only organization working exclusively on advancing the professional practice of wilderness stewardship. For more information, contact:

Society for Wilderness Stewardship
25903 N. Turkey Creek Road
Evergreen, CO 80439-5209
(303) 670-1642
info@wildernessstewardship.org
www.wildernessstewardship.org

Proceeds from this cookbook will help promote excellence in the professional practice of wilderness stewardship, science, and education.

WILDERNESS RANGER
▲▲▲
COOKBOOK

A Collection of Backcountry Recipes by
Bureau of Land Management, Forest Service, National Park Service,
and U.S. Fish and Wildlife Service Wilderness Rangers

50th anniversary of the signing of the Wilderness Act

Second Edition

VALERIE WIGGLESWORTH & RALPH SWAIN

Photographs by Bob Wick, Bureau of Land Management

FALCONGUIDES

GUILFORD, CONNECTICUT
HELENA, MONTANA
AN IMPRINT OF GLOBE PEQUOT PRESS

MIX
Paper from
responsible sources
FSC® C005010
www.fsc.org

50th anniversary logo courtesy of Wilderness50. Bureau of Land Management shield courtesy of the
Bureau of Land Management. Forest Service shield courtesy of the Forest Service. National Park
Service shield courtesy of the National Park Service. U.S. Fish and Wildlife Service shield courtesy
of U.S. Fish and Wildlife Service. Society for Wilderness Stewardship logo courtesy of Society for
Wilderness Stewardship. Osprey logo courtesy of Osprey Packs, Inc.

Photographs by Bob Wick, Bureau of Land Management, Sacramento, CA, unless otherwise credited
Map by Melissa Baker © Morris Book Publishing, LLC
Concept: Ralph Swain, Forest Service, Rocky Mountain Region
Editor: Valerie Wigglesworth

Library of Congress Cataloging-in-Publication Data

Wigglesworth, Valerie.
 Wilderness ranger cookbook : a collection of backcountry recipes by Bureau of Land Management,
Forest Service, National Park Service, and U.S. Fish and Wildlife Service Wilderness Rangers / Valerie
Wigglesworth and Ralph Swain ; photographs by Bob Wick, Bureau of Land Management — Second
edition.
     pages cm
   Summary: "A collection of trail-tested recipes from the Bureau of Land Management, National Park
Service, U.S. Fish and Wildlife Service, and Forest Service wilderness rangers, as well as wilderness
tips"— Provided by publisher.
 ISBN 978-1-4930-0629-8 (paperback)
1. Outdoor cooking. 2. Wilderness areas—United States. I. Swain, Ralph. II. Title.
TX823.B78 2014
641.5'78—dc23

2014015297

Printed in the United States of America

This cookbook is dedicated to the "down in the dirt" wilderness rangers and volunteers who have given their hearts and souls to protecting America's wildlands. The recipes included in this book are a combination of recipes from the first edition that remain our favorites today, as well as new recipes collected for this 50th Wilderness Anniversary edition cookbook. All the recipes are theirs—made with care, seasoned with experience, and perfected over time.

RECOGNITION

▲▲▲

This book was produced by the Society for Wilderness Stewardship and Osprey Packs, Inc. in cooperation with the four federal land management agencies that administer congressionally designated wilderness. The Society for Wilderness Stewardship, Bureau of Land Management, Forest Service, National Park Service, and U.S. Fish and Wildlife Service have partnered to commemorate the 50th anniversary of the signing of the Wilderness Act.

The development of this book was paid for in part by a grant from Osprey Packs, Inc.

Special thanks to Leanne Marten, Joe Ashor, Nancy Roeper, Erin Drake, Tim Devine, Ken Straley, Ben Lawhon, Tom Carlson, Diane Bedell, and Lee Lambert for their help on this book.

A big thanks also goes to our families, Betty and Sara Swain, and Eric, Elizabeth, and Alex Wigglesworth. This book couldn't have been done without their love and support.

CONTENTS

▲▲▲

National Wilderness Preservation System—May 2014

The National Wilderness Preservation System has 758 wilderness areas and encompasses nearly 110 million acres.

Designated Wilderness Areas

Bureau of Land Management   National Park Service

Forest Service   U.S. Fish and Wildlife Service

MAINE

Lake Superior

MINNESOTA

VERMONT

NEW HAMPSHIRE

WISCONSIN

Lake Huron

Lake Ontario

MASSACHUSETTS

NEW YORK

RHODE ISLAND

Lake Michigan

MICHIGAN

CONNECTICUT

Lake Erie

IOWA

PENNSYLVANIA

NEW JERSEY

OHIO

ILLINOIS

INDIANA

DELAWARE

MARYLAND

WEST VIRGINIA

VIRGINIA

MISSOURI

KENTUCKY

NORTH CAROLINA

TENNESSEE

ARKANSAS

SOUTH CAROLINA

MISSISSIPPI

GEORGIA

ALABAMA

Atlantic Ocean

LOUISIANA

FLORIDA

Gulf of Mexico

0   200 miles

HAWAII

0   100 miles

ABOUT THIS BOOK

Yes, we're doing it again!

Wilderness rangers from across America asked whether we would do a special 50th Wilderness Anniversary edition of the *Wilderness Ranger Cookbook* that we first produced in 1990. The answer was a resounding yes. How could we not?

The idea for the original cookbook started at a wilderness ranger workshop in Granby, Colorado, in the summer of 1989. The three-day training session brought seasonal and permanent wilderness staff together to exchange ideas about vexing management problems. Participants also practiced traditional skills, such as cutting with an ax and crosscut saw (chain saws are prohibited in wilderness) and packing with horses and llamas.

As an extra activity, rangers brought camp stoves to cook their favorite backcountry meals. This cook-off turned out to be one of the highlights of the workshop and was the catalyst for the first cookbook.

This edition expands on the original by including the best recipes from wilderness rangers and wildlife refuge managers from all four federal land management agencies: Bureau of Land Management, Forest Service, National Park Service, and U.S. Fish and Wildlife Service.

Start your day in the backcountry with some Sunrise Oatmeal, break for lunch to enjoy a Spinach and Black Bean Quesadilla, and cap off your evening with some Alpine Spaghetti.

But this cookbook is much more than just recipes for delicious backcountry cuisine. It is a celebration of what we do, why we care about wilderness, and why all Americans should be proud of this great nation and its enduring resource of wilderness. As part of the commemoration of the 50th anniversary of its signing, the Wilderness Act of 1964 is also included in its entirety for your reference.

We hope you enjoy this book as much as we do.

- Most recipes can be prepared in the field using a one-burner stove. Some recipes must be prepared at home and then packed for your backcountry trip. For many of the recipes, you can adjust the type and amount of ingredients based on what you have in your pack.

- Each recipe includes the name of the ranger who submitted it, the wilderness area where the ranger works now or has worked in the past, and the ranger's current hometown.

BREAKFAST

"In our digitally connected world, the value of wilderness—a place to literally unplug—has never been greater. Such a burden is lifted whenever I power down my computer and pick up my backpack."

—Michael Liang, Philadelphia, PA

Boulder Lake Granola
Michael Liang, North Cascades National Park

MAKES 6 CUPS

2 cups old-fashioned oats
1 cup shelled pumpkin seeds
1 cup shelled sunflower seeds
½ cup dried cranberries
½ cup unsalted cashews
⅓ cup brown sugar, packed
¼ cup flour
½ cup butter
⅓ cup maple syrup
½ cup peanut butter

To prepare at home: Preheat the oven to 350°F. In a large mixing bowl, combine all dried ingredients: oats, seeds, fruit, cashews, brown sugar, and flour. In a small saucepan, melt butter over medium-low heat. Stir in maple syrup and peanut butter until blended smoothly. Pour liquids into dry ingredients and mix until everything is moist and sticky. Once combined, spread mixture evenly on a metal cookie sheet and bake for 30 minutes. Every 10 minutes or so, stir the granola so that it roasts evenly (the edges will color first). Remove when everything is toasted and golden in color. Allow the granola to cool before storing in airtight containers. Keep a jar out for snacking and the rest in the freezer until your next hike.

"Wilderness is a place that not only wildlife, but also people, can find refuge and solitude. It's all of our responsibility to protect these special places to ensure future generations can witness nature in its purest form and have the opportunity to experience the magic of disconnecting from urbanized society."

—*Caitlin Smith, New Richmond, WI*

One-Pan Boundary Waters Burritos
Caitlin Smith, St. Croix Wetland Management District

MAKES 4 TO 6 SERVINGS

1 log of breakfast sausage
1 onion, chopped (optional)
1 bell pepper, chopped (optional)
8 eggs
8 ounces cheese
Salsa to taste
Sour cream to taste
1 package flour tortillas

Cook sausage until it is browned and cooked thoroughly. If desired, add chopped onion and bell pepper and cook until softened. Next, break the eggs into the pan of sausage and stir the mixture so the egg yolks break and are blended well. Just before the eggs are about scrambled, add the cheese. Add any seasoning that you have for flavor and spice. Salsa and sour cream are great additions if available. Spread a heaping spoonful onto each tortilla, roll the tortillas into burritos, and serve.

"Wilderness in its finest light is a meeting place for the development of relationships. It's where the simplicity and challenge of life allows us to learn the most about the natural system we're a part of, the people we are with, and the depth of our own selves."

—*Daniel Carver, Mosca, CO*

Ambassadorial Breakfast Gravel
Daniel Carver, Great Sand Dunes National Park and Preserve

MAKES 3 TO 4 SERVINGS

2 tablespoons margarine
2 cups Grape Nuts cereal
½ to ¾ cup peanut butter
½ cup chocolate hazelnut spread
Powdered milk
Filtered water

Melt margarine in a medium-size pot on medium-low heat. Add Grape Nuts and stir until combined. Move the cereal to the sides of the pot and glop the peanut butter into the center. Heat the peanut butter until softened, then stir into the cereal. Repeat the process with the chocolate hazelnut spread. Be sure to stir regularly to prevent burning. The mixture should be dark brown in color and taste similar to a peanut butter cup. Mix powdered milk with water as directed on package to make milk and then add to cereal to help cool.

Wilderness Designations

- First wilderness area: Gila Wilderness in New Mexico, administratively established by the Forest Service on June 3, 1924

- First U.S. Fish and Wildlife Service wilderness: Great Swamp National Wildlife Refuge Wilderness in New Jersey, designated on September 28, 1968

- First National Park Service wildernesses: Craters of the Moon National Wilderness Area in Idaho and Petrified Forest National Wilderness Area in Arizona, both designated on October 23, 1970

- First Forest Service wilderness (after the 1964 Wilderness Act): Scapegoat Wilderness in Montana, designated in 1972. (Scapegoat Wilderness is also the first citizen-initiated wilderness area to be created by Congress.)

- First Bureau of Land Management–managed wilderness: the Bear Trap Canyon unit of the Lee Metcalf Wilderness in Montana, designated on October 31, 1983

"I try to teach people to enjoy the area with an appropriate respect for its integrity as an ecosystem that is complete without human presence—we are just privileged guests. Wilderness to me should exist primarily for its own importance to the earth, not for any 'use' it may have to humanity."

—Monique H. Slipher, Baker, OR

Backcountry Scones
Monique H. Slipher, North Fork John Day Wilderness

2 cups flour
2 cups oats
2 tablespoons sugar
1 teaspoon salt
2 teaspoons baking soda
1 cup milk or ½ cup powdered milk mixed with 1 cup water
½ cup raisins, sunflower seeds, currants, nuts, or other fillings
½ cup vegetable oil

To prepare at home: Mix the dry ingredients together. Blend the oil in with a fork until the mixture looks like fine crumbs. Add 1 cup milk and pat into a large circle about ½-inch thick. Cut into small pieces and place on a greased cookie sheet. Bake 10–15 minutes at 425°F until golden brown.

To prepare in the field: Mix all ingredients (use ½ cup powdered milk mixed with water) except the oil. Then mix in the oil. Pat into a well-greased frying pan and score into sections. Cover and cook over low heat until done, about 20 minutes.

This logo commemorates the 50th anniversary of the National Wilderness Preservation System. To learn more, go to www.wilderness50th.org.

"Wilderness land is unique and valuable. We have an obligation to allow it to sustain itself and manage our own human impacts. How could we exist without it?"
—*Wendy Magwire, Granby, CO*

Blueberry Breakfast Cake
Wendy Magwire, Maroon Bells–Snowmass Wilderness

8 ounces canned blueberries, Oregon brand preferred
2 cups baking mix (such as Bisquick)
¼ cup powdered milk
2 tablespoons sugar
Dash of cinnamon
Water

Heat the blueberries in a skillet or other pan. While heating, mix baking mix, powdered milk, sugar, and cinnamon with enough water to make a thick batter. Drop large spoonfuls of batter onto the blueberries. Cover and let cook until the batter has become cakelike.

John Muir (1838–1914)— naturalist writer, founding president of Sierra Club, and early advocate of protecting public lands. *Courtesy of the National Park Service, John Muir National Historic Site (JOMU 3519)*

"Wilderness is home. It is how I connect with the natural world, with our heritage as humans capable of reflection, restraint, and compassion. Wildness provides energy and purpose to life, challenge, and hope for the future."

—Anne Dal Vera, Bayfield, CO

Couscous Delight
Anne Dal Vera, Weminuche Wilderness

MAKES 2 TO 3 SERVINGS

1 cup couscous
½ cup dried cranberries
3 packages apple cider mix
3 cups water
½ cup almond butter or peanut butter
½ cup apple butter

For the breakfast hot-cereal version: Cook the couscous, cranberries, and apple cider mix in a little more than 3 cups water to a soupy consistency. Ladle dollops of couscous, almond butter, and apple butter into a bowl or mug, stir, and enjoy.

For dessert or snack version: Cook the couscous, cranberries, and apple cider mix in 3 cups of water. Put half the couscous in the bottom of an 8-inch pie tin or skillet, and cool. When stiff, spread with almond butter. Cover with the remainder of the couscous. Spread apple butter on top. Serve when cooled a bit.

Variations: Add dried fruit, chopped nuts, powdered milk, brown sugar, salt, and/or cinnamon. This recipe can also be made with quinoa instead of couscous—it takes longer, but it has more protein.

"The Greek philosopher Pythagoras said, 'If there be light, then there is darkness; if cold, then heat; if height, depth also; if solid, then fluid; hardness and softness; roughness and smoothness; calm and tempest; prosperity and adversity; life and death.' Wilderness and civilization can be contrasted in the same way. They are opposites."

—Larry A. Jarvinen, Manistee, MI

Easy Granola
Larry A. Jarvinen, Nordhouse Dunes Wilderness

> 6 cups rolled oats
> 2 cups grated or shredded coconut
> 2 cups chopped nuts (any kind—almonds, cashews, walnuts)
> ⅔ cup sesame seeds or sunflower seeds
> ⅔ cup bran flakes
> ⅔ cup wheat germ
> ½ cup vegetable oil
> ½ cup honey (or molasses, sorghum, or maple syrup)
> 1 cup dried fruit
> Milk

To prepare at home: Roast each of the first six ingredients above separately in a 300°F oven until lightly toasted. Combine. Stir in the oil and honey thoroughly. Roast in a 250°F oven until golden brown. Store in an airtight container.

To serve in the field: Add dried fruit to cereal. Stir and serve with milk.

Sun-dried granola: In a big bowl, put 5 cups oatmeal. In a separate bowl, combine ½ cup honey, ½ cup hot water, ½ cup vegetable oil, 2 teaspoons vanilla. Add this to the oatmeal. Then add 1 cup sunflower seeds, 1 cup sesame seeds, 1 cup flax seeds, 1 cup grated coconut, ¾ cup chopped dried fruit. Mix well and spread somewhere flat to dry (at least two days). Serve with milk when ready.

"To enjoy creation is to enjoy the creator. To enjoy the creator is to know God and view the beauty of His handiwork in creation and in our lives. Wilderness is an experience where we become engulfed in the bond between peace and beauty."
—*Walter (Sym) Terhune, Florence, WI*

Egg in the Nest
Walter (Sym) Terhune, Whisker Lake Wilderness

MAKES 1 SERVING

1 tablespoon bacon grease, butter, or shortening
1 piece of bread
1 egg

Over moderate heat, melt grease, butter, or shortening in a frying pan. The grease should cover the bottom of the pan. Cut out a hole in the center of the bread the size of an egg yolk. Place the bread in the pan of hot grease. Break the entire egg over the hole in the bread so that the egg yolk sits in hole. Fry the egg and bread to personal preference, flipping once, and serve.

Aldo Leopold, 1887–1948—author of *A Sand County Almanac and Sketches Here and There* and a leader in early wilderness stewardship. *Courtesy of the Aldo Leopold Foundation Archives*

"The United States without wilderness would be like living without sunshine."
—Rebecca E. Ondov, MT

Twigs and Rocks
Rebecca E. Ondov, Scapegoat Wilderness

    4 cups blueberry granola
    ¼ cup oat bran
    ¼ cup chopped walnuts
    4 cups raw quick oats
    ¼ cup slivered almonds
    1 cup raisins or currants
    Brown sugar to taste
    Evaporated milk to taste
    Water

Combine the first six ingredients. Add brown sugar and milk to cereal as desired. I prefer to eat it cold, but for a change of pace, you can cook it up like hot cereal. Add 1 part cereal to ⅔ parts water and heat until warm.

Variations: Add dried bananas or peaches.

"When viewing the Glen Canyon after the dam was built, Edward Abbey said, 'Once it was different there. I know, for I was one of the lucky few . . .' When I view the wilderness, I say, 'I am one of the lucky few. I will keep it different here.'"
—*Jerry Craghead, Burns, CO*

Eggs McSanchez
Jerry Craghead, Holy Cross Wilderness

MAKES 1 SERVING

2 eggs
2 strips of beef jerky
2 jalapeño peppers, diced
Tabasco Sauce to taste
1 tortilla

The night before: Beat the eggs. Tear the jerky into little pieces, and peel and chop the jalapeños. Add those to the eggs. Then add enough Tabasco to extinguish any flames caused by the jalapeños. Mix and let the mixture sit overnight.

In the morning: Cook all of the runny stuff over low heat in a pan until it's well done. Scoop it into the tortilla, add a little more Tabasco, and hit the trail.

Howard Zahniser (1906–1964)— executive director of The Wilderness Society. He proposed the first wilderness bill in 1956. *Courtesy Wilderness.net*

"My personal wilderness philosophy? Do it with flair!"

—Dave Atwood, Orleans, CA

Griddle Cakes
Dave Atwood, Marble Mountain Wilderness

1¼ cups sifted flour
2 teaspoons baking powder
½ teaspoon baking soda
1 tablespoon sugar
½ teaspoon salt
1 beaten egg
1 cup buttermilk
2 tablespoons vegetable oil or melted shortening

Mix the dry ingredients. Mix in the egg, buttermilk, and oil just until moistened. The batter will be thick and lumpy. Pour onto an ungreased griddle, about ¼ cup at a time. Cook over medium heat until brown. Flip. Cook until done and serve.

"Inspired people can change the world. This world needs a lot of change. By pre-serving pieces of our past in wilderness, maybe we can find inspiration and vital information to help mend the torn earth."

—Michael McCurdy, Seward, AK

New Granola, Jamie Style
Michael McCurdy, Moose Plains National Wildlife Refuge

1½ cups margarine
3 3-inch squares of shredded wheat
½ cup oats
1 cup peanut butter
¾ cup honey or sugar
⅓–½ cup powdered milk
½ cup raisins
¼ cup peanuts
¼ cup assorted nuts (use your favorites) or cashews
½ cup sunflower seeds
1 teaspoon cinnamon

Melt margarine in a large pan. Brown the shredded wheat. Add the oats and brown. Mix in the peanut butter, honey or sugar, powdered milk, and raisins. Cook over medium heat and stir frequently until the raisins plump. Add the nuts, sunflower seeds, and cinnamon (sometimes I brown the nuts separately). If it's too dry, add more margarine or powdered milk reconstituted with water.

"Today's wild places represent areas that native people used to call home. A home where the creator provided everything needed to live healthy and happy, in balance with all things. So let's offer these integral cultural groups more opportunities to engage in wilderness, and let's provide our dedicated field-going workforce full-time employment."

—Greg F. Hansen, Mesa, AZ

Superstition Surprise
Greg F. Hansen, Superstition Wilderness

MAKES 3 TO 4 SERVINGS

2 cups oatmeal, instant or slow-cooking
⅓ cup raisins
⅓ cup mixed, chopped nuts (use your favorites)
½ cup brown sugar
¼ teaspoon cinnamon
¼ teaspoon nutmeg
¼ teaspoon allspice
¾ cup powdered milk (optional)
½ to 1 cup water (just enough to cover cereal)

Mix all ingredients except water in a sealable bag before hitting the trail. When the breakfast bell rings, pour boiling water over your Superstition Surprise and cover the pot. Wait about 2 minutes, and you're ready to chow down.

"Wilderness reflects the different cultures of man. We must not lose our love for this land as it provides for our health, well-being, and self-renewal. To understand wilderness and marvel at its beauty and value is to understand ourselves."

—*Don Duff, Salt Lake City, UT*

Sunrise Oatmeal
Don Duff, Deseret Peak Wilderness

MAKES 1 SERVING

¾ cup oatmeal
¼ cup dried bananas or raisins
Cinnamon to taste
1 tablespoon powdered milk
¼ cup chopped apple (optional)
1 cup water

Add all ingredients to water in a pot. Bring to a boil, reduce heat, and cook for 2 minutes. Serve.

The Wilderness Act was signed into law September 3, 1964, by President Lyndon B. Johnson. *Courtesy of the National Archives*

LUNCH

"Wild can mean unruly or crazy, as in wild hair or a wild day. But it is sometimes used to describe places perceived to be unspoiled by humans. Before disturbance from an outside world, native people had no word for wild. Now our tamed domestic landscapes provide stark contrast to native landscapes, and so we invented the term wilderness. I believe there is something rooted deeply within our souls that, if acknowledged, craves connection with the native world and spawns a need; perhaps to belong, at least for a moment, to a place where the word 'wild' makes no sense."

—*Pauline Drobney, Prairie City, IA*

Savanna Sojourn Sandwich

Pauline Drobney, U.S. Fish and Wildlife Service Midwest Region prairies and savannas

MAKES 1 SERVING

1 tablespoon horseradish
1 tablespoon mayonnaise (optional)
2 slices hearty whole grain bread
1 tablespoon favorite jam
1 apple, sliced horizontally
1 slice swiss, smoked gouda, or favorite cheese
2 slices shaved ham

Spread horseradish (and mayonnaise if desired) on one slice of bread, and jam on the other slice. Place apple pieces on horseradish, followed by cheese and ham. Place bread with jam on top.

Variations: Replace bread with pita bread. Try dried fruit or other meat, or add nuts.

"I value wilderness because these special places are free from anthropogenic intrusions such as lights, noise, machinery, and perceived safety. For me, wilderness areas provide for true restoration and solemn reflection among primeval nature."
—Derrick Taff, State College, PA

Spinach and Black Bean Quesadillas
Derrick Taff, Rocky Mountain National Park

MAKES 2 SERVINGS

4 ounces water
3 ounces dehydrated black beans
3 ounces fresh spinach leaves
4 ounces of Oaxaca cheese (Parmesan is lighter in your pack but doesn't taste as good)
4 flour tortillas
1 ounce salsa (spiciness to taste)

Prepack all items to eliminate packaging waste prior to your departure. Premeasure items so food won't be wasted in the backcountry. Bring water to a boil and hydrate the black beans. Drain the excess water (and remember to leave no trace when disposing of water). Turn the stove burner to low, add the spinach and cheese to the cooked black beans. Stir until the cheese is melted. Place a tortilla on your plate and add the cooked ingredients on top. Add salsa to taste. Top with a second tortilla.

Memorable Words on Wilderness

"Wilderness can be appreciated only by contrast, and solitude understood only when we have been without it."
—Sigurd F. Olson, author and conservation leader

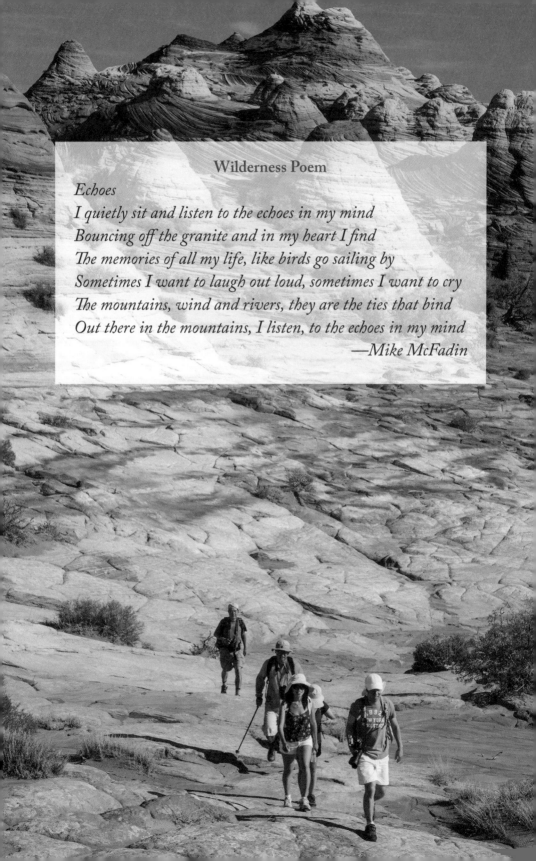

Wilderness Poem

Echoes
I quietly sit and listen to the echoes in my mind
Bouncing off the granite and in my heart I find
The memories of all my life, like birds go sailing by
Sometimes I want to laugh out loud, sometimes I want to cry
The mountains, wind and rivers, they are the ties that bind
Out there in the mountains, I listen, to the echoes in my mind
                                        —Mike McFadin

"Those of us who choose this work do it out of passion. The pay alone isn't enough to tempt anyone who doesn't love the way of life we lead. It is an honor to manage public lands and a privilege to work in the high country we call home."
—*Mike McFadin, Weaverville, CA*

Hummus Bagel
Mike McFadin, Trinity River Management Unit

MAKES 4 TO 5 SERVINGS

½ cup sun-dried tomatoes
¼ cup bacon bits
2 cups powdered hummus
½ cup salt-and-vinegar chips (optional; Tim's Cascade Snacks preferred)
2 to 4 tablespoons water
4 or 5 bagels

To prepare at home: Finely chop sun-dried tomatoes. In a bowl mix the sun-dried tomatoes, bacon bits, and powdered hummus. For an especially zippy mix, add crushed salt-and-vinegar chips. Divide the mixture into four or five resealable baggies (depending on how much hummus you want per bagel).

To serve in the field: As soon as you sit down to eat, take out a bag of the hummus mixture and add enough water to turn it into paste, zipping the bag up and squishing it around to mix. Let it set for about 10 minutes while you eat other stuff, pump water through a filter, or doctor your feet. Split a bagel in half and lay it on a clean surface such as your knee, a log, a rock or the back of your pack. Cut or bite a hole in one corner of your baggie and pipe the hummus onto bagel halves. Squirting mixture directly into your mouth is also acceptable.

Variations: Add salami, pepperoni, or some other type of healthy salt, nitrate, and protein substance to the top. Add 1 tablespoon cayenne pepper to the mix for Hot Hummus, 2 tablespoons for Holy Smokes Hummus, and ¼ cup for Fire in the Hole Hummus. Add Italian seasoning mix for Pizza Pie on the Fly Hummus. Or add ¼ cup brown sugar, ¼ cup chopped coconut, 2 tablespoons crushed red pepper flakes, and ¼ cup crushed peanuts for Kinda Thai on the Fly Hummus.

"I never met a trail crew volunteer that I did not like."

—Bill Goslin, Stevensville, MT

Hummus and Veggie Roll-up
Bill Goslin, Selway–Bitterroot Wilderness

MAKES 3 SERVINGS OVER 3 DAYS

1 red pepper, pre-cored
2 medium carrots
1 celery stalk
10 ounces red pepper–flavored hummus stored in a no-leak food
    container
6 tortillas

To prepare at home: Chop up vegetables and seal in a no-leak food container.

To serve in the field: Spread the hummus on a tortilla and top with veggies. Roll up the tortilla and eat. The ingredients hold up well for several days in the summer heat.

Variations: Add other vegetables.

"While in a wilderness experience, I am grounded by the solitude, natural features, and surroundings. When I return from a wilderness experience, I soar with renewed spirit and mind/body rejuvenation."

—Chuck Houghten, Portland, OR

Backcountry Bagel Sandwich

Chuck Houghten, U.S. Fish and Wildlife Service Pacific Region

MAKES 1 SERVING

1 bagel of choice (multigrain is preferred)
1 can quality smoked sardines (in water, oil, or—the best—mustard sauce)
1 clove garlic
1 slice sharp cheddar cheese (or another favorite cheese; optional)

Slice the bagel in half. Add two or three whole sardines to one bagel half. Slice the garlic and layer over the sardines. Add a slice of your favorite cheese and top with remaining bagel half. Be sure to have a small container or plastic bag to carry out the empty sardine can.

Memorable Words on Wilderness

"It is not good for man to be kept perforce at all times in the presence of his species. A world from which solitude is extirpated is a very poor ideal. Solitude, in the sense of being often alone, is essential to any depth of meditation or of character; and solitude in the presence of natural beauty and grandeur is the cradle of thoughts and aspirations which are not only good for the individual but which society could ill do without."

—John Stuart Mill, Principles of Political Economy

"Wilderness is a pathway to truth. The more time we spend in the wilderness, the more we learn about what is really significant about life and ourselves. Wilderness gives us a clear-eyed perspective, free of clutter. Life's major decisions should be made in the mountains, the desert, the forests, or in any other wild place."

—*Jim Bradley, Enterprise, OR*

The Eagle Cap Club
Jim Bradley, Eagle Cap Wilderness

MAKES 5 TO 10 SERVINGS, DEPENDING ON HOW HUNGRY YOU ARE

1 dry salami (the hottest and spiciest you can find)
1 pound sharp cheddar cheese
1 box of your favorite crackers

This favorite trail lunch, which is fast, easy, and tasty, is named in honor of the Eagle Cap Wilderness. Slice the cheese and salami. Place between two crackers to make a sandwich. The ingredients can easily survive a ten-day hike in the heat.

Wilderness Facts

- Nationwide, there are 758 wilderness areas totaling nearly 110 million acres, or 5 percent of all U.S. land.

- The largest wilderness area, at more than 9 million acres, is in Wrangell–St. Elias National Park in Alaska.

- The largest contiguous wilderness outside of Alaska is the 2.3-million-acre Frank Church–River of No Return Wilderness in Idaho.

- The largest legislative wilderness outside of Alaska is the Death Valley Wilderness in California and Nevada, encompassing more than 3.1 million acres.

- The smallest wilderness is the 5.5-acre Pelican Island in Florida.

"Everyone benefits from wilderness, even those who may have never set foot in one. So it's important that everyone understand it needs to be protected and preserved."
—Becky Boyer, Munising, MI

Bagel Break
Becky Boyer, Big Island Lake Wilderness

MAKES 1 SERVING

1 bagel
1 package of cream cheese
1 cucumber, thinly sliced
1 handful alfalfa sprouts

Cut the bagel in half. Spread cream cheese over both halves, using an amount that will satisfy your personal taste. Place cucumber slices and alfalfa sprouts on top. Put bagel halves together and enjoy.

"Wilderness frees me in a way no other thing on earth can do. Wilderness is primal, wild, and natural; it allows me to connect with life itself. It's not always about the physical journey. For me it's all about arriving at my mental destination. Wilderness gets me there."

—*Justin Loxley, Flagstaff, AZ*

Loxley's Backcountry Quesadilla
Justin Loxley, Coconino National Forest

MAKES 3 TO 4 SERVINGS

2 teaspoons olive oil

4 8- to 10-inch flour tortillas (corn also works)

10 to 12 ounces prepackaged white chicken meat (can also substitute tuna, trout, or salmon)

1 small bag of shredded cheddar cheese or a half block of Velveeta (if backpacking)

1 cup fresh cilantro, chopped

1 small can green chiles (can be dehydrated)

1 cup dehydrated refried beans

1 Roma tomato, sliced

1 small cucumber, sliced

1 medium avocado, sliced

Salt, pepper, and hot sauce to taste

Lightly oil one side of a tortilla and place in a pan. Spread ½ of chicken meat evenly on the tortilla and then cover with half of the cheese, cilantro, and green chile strips. Cover with a second tortilla, and then layer with beans, sliced tomato, cucumber, and avocado. Follow up with a third tortilla; top this with remaining chicken, cheese, cilantro, and green chile strips. Top all this with one more tortilla, lightly oiled on top. Cook on low/slow heat for 3 to 4 minutes on one side, then flip and cook some more, achieving a lightly browned surface on both sides. Cover the pan to help melt the cheese and wake up the cilantro and chiles. Add salt, pepper, and hot sauce to taste. A truly utopian experience for your belly.

Note: This works best with a Teflon pan rather than a cook pot since you have to brown both sides of the quesadilla. If only a cook pot is available, make the layers as instructed above, wrap in foil, and place in the cook pot. If you have no pot, set the foil on cool fire coals.

"Whether laying fresh tracks or following an ancient trail, being in wilderness is like coming home."

—*Jenner Harsha, Colter Bay, WY*

Tropical Vacation Quinoa
Jenner Harsha, Grand Teton National Park

SERVES 1 HUNGRY RANGER

⅛ cup shredded dried coconut
½ cup dry quinoa
1 cup water
4 slices dried mango, diced
½ avocado, cubed
¼ teaspoon cumin
Salt and pepper to taste

Toast the coconut at home over medium heat, stirring constantly until browned (just a minute or two). Cool and store in a sandwich bag. Alternatively, you can do the same over a camp stove. Bring quinoa and 1 cup of water to a boil, reduce heat, and simmer for 10 to 15 minutes. Toss in the mango; turn off the heat and let sit for a few minutes to plump the fruit. Stir toasted coconut, avocado, cumin, salt, and pepper into quinoa. Mix well.

Variations: Add diced tomato, freeze-dried corn, chopped nuts, and red pepper flakes.

"We should begin to rethink our priorities, renew our commitment to preserving our wildernesses from unalterable damages and restore our public image to that of the caretakers of our forests."

—William DellaRocco, Dolores, CO

Sautéed Chanterelles
William DellaRocco, Lizard Head Wilderness

MAKES 1 SERVING

2 handfuls of chanterelles
¼ onion, diced
½ clove of garlic, chopped fine
Dash of soy sauce (optional)

Cook chanterelles, onions, and garlic on low heat in a pan. The key to not overcooking this delicate mushroom is to periodically remove the pan from the cook stove. If the garlic is turning brown or the onions are smoking, snatch the dish from heat. Slowly fry until the chanterelles soften. Add soy sauce and serve.

Mushroom Identification

- Accuracy of identification is essential to not confuse a poisonous mushroom with an edible one.

- Be meticulous when identifying. If in doubt, don't eat it.

- Eat only healthy mushrooms.

- Mushrooms should always be cooked before eating.

- When trying a new variety, eat only a small amount and save a few raw pieces in case of misidentification.

- Eat only one type at a time.

- Remember that different people can have different reactions to the same mushroom.

"Many years ago I discovered the presence of something very wonderful in the forest. It gives me peace of mind unlike anything else in my life. I've spent many an hour listening to and thinking about whatever this is and still cannot describe it to mere mortals. They'll have to discover it for themselves. But then again, I'm afraid most major organized religions would go bankrupt if everyone found out what really exists in the wilderness."

—*Bill C. Self, Ogden, UT*

Let'seatus Some Boletus (Sautéed Mushrooms)
Bill C. Self, High Uintas Wilderness

MAKES 1 TO 2 SERVINGS

1 cup sliced boletus mushrooms (use canned mushrooms if not familiar with wild varieties)
1 stick of butter
4 ounces V8 Juice
Salt, pepper, and garlic powder to taste
2 dashes of red wine
2 to 4 slices of French bread

Brush the organic debris from the mushrooms and peel the pores from the undersurface of the cap. Then slice them vertically about ¼-inch thick. Heat up the pan until the butter is barely sizzling. Sauté the mushrooms for about 2 minutes, turning them as they begin to darken. Add V8, spices, and wine. Stir while cooking for 2 more minutes. Do not overcook. Use the leftover sauce for dipping French bread.

Note: When selecting mushrooms, make sure you know what you are doing. Boletus mushrooms have pores under the caps rather than gills. They have large crowns (golden/brown with a slight white cracking in the mature stages). The stems are whitish gray with slight feathering. The buttons are best for eating, but are the host for a small fly, so they must be carefully cleaned.

"Wilderness is about the future. Wilderness provides for clean air, clean water, and ecosystems in a natural state. Add in the human need for open spaces, and you realize that we have set up a system of lands that will provide much-needed resources in the future. For my children and generations to come, I am proud of what we have done."

—Jimmy Gaudry, Atlanta, GA

Jerk Jambalaya

Jimmy Gaudry, Forest Service, Southern Region

MAKES 1 SERVING

1 package of spicy beef jerky
1 package of sun-dried tomatoes
1 package of precooked jambalaya mix, Zatarain's preferred
Bread or a tortilla

Cut the jerky and tomatoes into very small pieces. Start cooking the jambalaya mix as instructed. Add sun-dried tomatoes right away so they soften up. Once the jambalaya is heated, add the jerky pieces. Serve with bread or put on a tortilla for a jerk jambalaya burrito.

"I became a wilderness ranger because I wanted to play a part in the 'on-the-ground' management of this beautiful lake country wilderness, and to know first-hand its mystique and appreciate its wonders and challenges."

—Yvonne Schmidt, Cook, MN

Bongko Bean Spread

Yvonne Schmidt, Boundary Waters Canoe Area Wilderness

1¼ cups cooked garbanzo beans
¼ teaspoon dried parsley
¼ teaspoon chili powder
⅛ teaspoon cumin
⅛ teaspoon salt
Dash of garlic
Crackers or chips
Vegetable oil

To prepare at home: Mash garbanzos or put through a food mill, ricer, or blender until they make a paste. Add spices and stir well. Store in an airtight, heavy plastic container.

To serve in the field: Eat with crackers or chips. If the bean spread seems too dry, add a little vegetable oil.

Special Conditions of the Wilderness Act

- Aircraft or motorboat use may be permitted where established prior to designation as a wilderness.

- Livestock grazing, where established prior to wilderness designation, shall be permitted to continue subject to reasonable regulations.

- Hunting, fishing, and trapping may be allowed under state and federal laws, although hunting is prohibited in most national parks.

- Outfitting and guiding services may be allowed under special use permits that meet wilderness purposes.

"This lunch was shared by a smokejumper high in the Rocky Mountains. The wilderness and backcountry are precious national resources. Firefighters have a special partnership with the wilderness, protecting it for future generations."

—Ron Myers, Beulah, CO

Smokejumper Spam

Ron Myers, Greenhorn Mountain Wilderness

MAKES 1 SERVING

1 slice of Spam
1 single-serving can of fruit cocktail

Take a relatively clean shovel and get it very hot on a bed of coals. Take a slice of Spam and throw it on the shovel blade. Cook until seared, then turn the Spam over. Sear the other side and then pour the fruit cocktail directly over the seared Spam. The fruit cocktail will caramelize with the Spam. The combination is beyond description, especially when you are in the backcountry.

"Being in the wilderness brings perspective upon everything in life and reminds us of what's important."

—*Paul Sever, Redway, CA*

Lost Coast Intertidal Burrito

Paul Sever, King Range National Conservation Area

MAKES 1 SERVING

1 cup water
2 handfuls of dehydrated beans (black, pinto or refried)
Cheese of your choice, two to four slices
1 ripe avocado
Hot sauce to taste
Chicken, dried beef, or textured vegetable protein (optional)
1 large tortilla

Bring water to a boil in a pot. Add the beans, reduce heat to the lowest setting, and stir until the water is well absorbed (a few minutes). Cut the cheese into slices and slice the avocado. Combine all ingredients on a tortilla and wrap it up.

Variation: If you want to add instant rice, cook the rice first. Then add 1 cup water and the beans to that same pot, and cook as directed.

SNACKS

"As human beings we are works in progress, and our diverse life experiences continue to build and shape our characters and identities. I believe that sharing in the awesome responsibility and incredible privilege of wilderness stewardship, for the use and enjoyment by present and future generations, to be one of the finest life experiences of all."

—*Eric Flood, Alpine, AZ*

Blue Range Gorp
Eric Flood, Apache–Sitgreaves National Forests

MAKES 1 LARGE BATCH GOOD FOR 8 DAYS OF HIKING

1 cup dark chocolate M&M's
1 cup honey mustard and onion–flavored pretzels (Snyder's brand preferred)
1 cup jumbo raisins
1 cup cashews
1 cup dried blueberries
1 cup honey-roasted peanuts
1 cup dried cherries
1 cup cocoa-dusted almonds
1 cup dried cranberries
1 cup shelled pistachios
1 cup glazed pecans

To prepare at home: Combine all ingredients in a one-gallon resealable bag and shake gently to mix. Freeze for long-term storage.

Variations: Substitute different pretzel flavors: Bacon and cheddar, jalapeño, cheddar cheese, or buffalo wing are all possibilities.

"Wilderness demonstrates and preserves the diversity of America's landscapes. At Lake Mead National Recreation Area, the nine wilderness areas provide peace and solitude just 30 minutes from the Las Vegas strip. I enjoy seeing visitors escape to the park's wilderness to recreate among the colorful geological desert formations and the petroglyphs that share the cultural history of America's past."

—Christie Vanover, Boulder City, NV

Black Canyon Baconuts

Christie Vanover, Lake Mead National Recreation Area

MAKES 2 TO 3 CUPS

5 slices bacon
½ cup brown sugar
1 tablespoon chili powder
2 tablespoons Dijon mustard
4 cups mixed nuts
½ teaspoon kosher salt

To prepare at home: Preheat the oven to 400°F. Chop the bacon and mix with the remaining ingredients in a large bowl. Spread the mixture onto a foil-lined pan or baking sheet. Bake for about 18 minutes. Remove from the oven and spread onto a sheet of wax paper to cool. Break into pieces and pack in a resealable bag.

"You are a visitor who does not remain . . . leave no trace."
                    —Bob Oset, Hamilton, MT

Vitamin Balls
Bob Oset, Selway–Bitterroot Wilderness

1 cup honey
1 cup peanut butter
½ cup wheat germ
1 cup soymilk powder
½ cup carob powder
1 cup sesame seeds

To prepare at home: Mix all ingredients together. Separate into bite-size pieces and chill. Store in an airtight container, throw into your pack, and hit the trail.

Frozen Olives

From Madeline Tighe, who works in Grand Canyon National Park in Arizona: "Olives are high in salt and make for a great snack in hot weather. Drain your favorite olives, place them in a sealed baggie and freeze. Before hitting the trail, place the frozen olives near other food items or water in your pack to help keep them cool. The olives can be eaten thawed or frozen. Just remember, if you pack the pits in, pack the pits out."

Volosina/Shutterstock

Wildflowers

Wildflowers should be left for others to enjoy.

Wilderness Facts

- The National Wilderness Preservation System encompasses 5 percent of the entire United States—an area slightly larger than the state of California.

- If you don't count the wilderness in Alaska, then only about 2.7 percent of the contiguous United States is wilderness—an area about the size of Minnesota.

"I love the scenery, fresh air, and peaceful tranquility that the wilderness offers."
—Kathy Rydberg, Pecos, NM

Kathy's Magic Popcorn
Kathy Rydberg, Pecos Wilderness

MAKES 1 SERVING

1½ tablespoons olive oil
¼ cup popcorn
1½ tablespoons brewer's yeast
Salt to taste

Pour oil into a backpack pot. With 3 kernels of popcorn at the bottom and the cover on, turn the stove on high. After the 3 kernels pop, pour the rest of the popcorn into the pot. Just before the popping stops, remove the pot from the stove. Sprinkle the brewer's yeast over the popcorn. Add salt if desired.

DINNER

"At first, I took wilderness for granted because I didn't know any better. Now I hope I can be counted as one who has helped to secure wilderness in our future by utilizing the small or large means available to me."

—Ros Wu, Pagosa Springs, CO

Weminuche Burrito
Ros Wu, Weminuche and South San Juan Wildernesses

MAKES 2 TO 4 BURRITOS

1 small to medium onion, chopped
Other vegetables, chopped (bell pepper, zucchini, etc.; optional)
½ cup Hatch green chiles (fresh green chiles diced and frozen at home
    before the trip are best, but canned will work)
1 can of your favorite beans
Flour tortillas
Cooking oil or butter
1 large tomato, diced
Cheddar or Monterey Jack cheese, cut into small pieces (amount is your
    choice)
1 avocado
Salt and pepper to taste

Sauté the onion and other veggies in a pot or pan until soft and add chiles. Add the beans and cook until heated through. Then, if desired, panfry the tortillas with cooking oil or butter. Fill tortillas with cooked veggies, diced tomato, cheese, avocado, salt, and pepper to taste. Roll into burritos and enjoy.

Variations: Use a couple of cloves of garlic instead of the onion. Wrap the burrito in foil and put it on the edge of your fire to melt the cheese.

Memorable Words on Wilderness

"Something will have gone out of us as a people if we ever let the remaining wilderness be destroyed."
—Wallace Stegner, author and wilderness advocate

"It is impossible to adequately describe what wilderness means to me. People spend their entire lives trying to capture that feeling and express it. I feel privileged to have had the opportunity to spend so much of life working with talented and impassioned people in some of this country's special undeveloped places."

—*Kirstin Heins, Bishop, CA*

Red Lentil Curry with Creamed Coconut
Kirstin Heins, Bureau of Land Management, Bishop Field Office

> 4 ounces (½ cup) red lentils
> 10 ounces (1¼ cup) water
> ¼ cup dried tart cherries
> 2 teaspoons curry seasoning (depending on the blend it will typically include other spices)
> 1 teaspoon garlic powder
> Red chili powder to taste (optional)
> 3.5 ounces unsweetened creamed coconut (half of a 7-ounce vacuum-sealed package)
> Additional water for lentils and coconut, as needed
> Chopped peanuts or cashews to taste
> Salt and pepper to taste

To prepare at home: Rinse, sort, and drain lentils and put them in a sealed plastic bag. If you will be traveling in a cool environment, chop the creamed coconut into smaller pieces and bag it as well; in a warm environment the coconut will have a creamy texture and that efficiency will not be necessary.

To prepare in the field: Add lentils to 10 ounces of water and bring to a boil. Simmer for five minutes; cover and set aside while the lentils continue to hydrate. Standard cooking time for lentils is about 25 minutes or until tender, but you save fuel if you cover and let them hydrate in the hot water. After about 15 minutes of hydration, return the pot of lentils to the stove and bring it to a boil. Once boiling, add the dried cherries to hydrate them. Add the curry seasoning, garlic powder, and red chili powder, if desired. Stir in the creamed coconut. If it's still firm, it will break down in the heat. Add additional water as needed to dissolve the coconut. Cook the mixture to your desired consistency. Top with peanuts or cashews for texture, and add salt and pepper to taste.

Variations: In addition to, or in lieu of, the dried cherries, add fresh vegetables (early in a trip or on a short trip), dehydrated vegetables, or other dried fruit, such as mango or raisins. For additional protein, add vacuum-sealed chicken or fish.

"This recipe is a collaborative concoction arising from the imaginations of the Shaboygan Sundowners, a backpacking team of five people and three dogs that hiked the Colorado Trail in 2003. What started as a way to utilize all the food left in our packs before the next day's re-ration turned into a trail meal of choice."
—*Steve Chesterton, Rockville, MD*

Stormtrooper Surprise
Steve Chesterton, Wilderness and Wild and Scenic Rivers, Forest Service, Washington Office

About 4 quarts of water
16-ounce package of macaroni shells
1 red pepper, chopped
1 packet instant garlic mashed potatoes
8 ounces sharp cheddar cheese
Cayenne pepper and garlic powder to taste

Bring pot of water to boil and add macaroni shells and chopped red pepper. Once cooked, dump nearly all of the excess water, leaving just enough to hydrate the mashed potatoes. Return to the stove and add the instant mashed potatoes and cheese. Mix well. Add cayenne pepper and garlic powder to taste.

Preparing for Your Trip

- When buying packs, clothing, and tents, select earth-toned colors that blend with the natural surroundings.

- Obtain information about the various areas you will be exploring and the regulations governing their use well ahead of time.

- Repackage food in plastic bags or other lightweight containers. Avoid packing cans or glass bottles into the wilderness. And remember, if you pack it in, pack it out.

"Wilderness means to me a place to be in solitude and to learn the truth about where I come from. It reflects back to me truth about balance, simplicity, and acceptance. It gives me a glimpse of how to live in the most basic way. It's an opportunity to serve as a steward, respecting and protecting its primeval character. Wilderness has its own story, with all its mysteries that will never fully be revealed to man. Our best hope is to acknowledge our limitations and leave wilderness to do as it will, taking care to notice, learn, and leave be."

—Noel Gill, Silver City, NM

Divine Swine (Stuffed Pork Burger)
Noel Gill, Blue Range Primitive Area and Bear Wallow Wilderness

MAKES 2 TO 3 BURGERS

½ medium-size apple
2 jalapeños (remove seeds)
½ cup almonds
2 garlic cloves
1 tablespoon ginger root
2 tablespoons almond butter
Salt, pepper, and cumin to taste
1 pound organic pork

Stuffing: Finely dice the apple, jalapeños, almonds, and garlic. Finely shred the ginger root. Combine these ingredients with the almond butter, adding salt, pepper, and cumin to taste.

Patties: Season the pork with salt, pepper, and cumin to taste. Form the pork into 4 to 6 thin patties. Place half of the patties in a frying pan. Spread stuffing on each patty, leaving the edges free. Attach upper patties to lower patties. Fry, flip, and serve.

"The staff, volunteers, and friends work hard to continue the vision and mission of the refuge namesake, Ding Darling. Getting people outdoors and educating them about the importance of wildlife protection is so important to cultivating our future generations of conservation stewards."

—Birgie Miller Vertesch, Sanibel Island, FL

Pan-Fried Potato Chip Fish
Birgie Miller Vertesch, J. N. "Ding" Darling National Wildlife Refuge

MAKES 6 SERVINGS

6 fresh fish fillets with skin removed (sea trout, sheepshead, snapper, and
     flounder all work well)
4 cups finely crushed potato chips (crackers also work well)
1 egg (if you have it) or melted butter
2 tablespoons water
Oil or butter for frying
Mustard sauce or tartar sauce (optional)

Rinse the fish and pat dry with paper towels. Leave it as full fillets or cut into serving size pieces. Crush the potato chips in their bag making them as small as you can. In a shallow dish, mix the egg and water. If you don't have an egg, melt some butter in a bowl. Dip the fish into the egg mixture or melted butter. Toss into the crushed potato chips and coat completely. In a frying pan, heat up about ¼ inch of oil or butter. Add the fish in a single layer and fry until golden. Turn carefully and fry the other side until the fish begins to flake when tested with a fork. Depending on the thickness of the fillets, allow 4 to 5 minutes per side. Drain on paper towels. Eat with mustard sauce or tartar sauce.

"As a species, our roots are in wilderness. It's a reservoir of clean air, clear water, fish, wildlife, serenity, beauty, and reality. It wakes us up from the confused, dreamy mental state our society inspires. We need wilderness, and we need to save and preserve what we have left—not only for ourselves, but as a long-overdue acknowledgment of the right of other living things to live their own lives for themselves."
—Jon R. Herman, Roslyn, WA

Pilaf de Résistance
Jon R. Herman, Alpine Lakes Wilderness

2¼ cups water
1 cup quick brown rice
½ cup instant refried beans
1 small can chicken or turkey meat
¼ cup diced green pepper
¼ cup chopped celery
2 tablespoons diced onion
½ teaspoon diced garlic or garlic powder
1 teaspoon dried celery
¼ teaspoon salt
1 slice cheddar cheese

Bring water to a boil. Add the rice. Cover and simmer for 10 minutes. Then add all ingredients except the cheese. Simmer and stir occasionally for 5 minutes. Add the cheese and set aside with the cover on the pot. Serve when cheese is melted.

"I value wilderness because it's given us a fun topic to argue about . . . those who want to save it versus those who want to develop it. What wilderness means to me is the preservation of wildness, and there is no bigger conflict in the American value system."

—R. Patrick Cook, Darrington, WA

Hobo Stew
R. Patrick Cook, Boulder River Wilderness

MAKES 2 SERVINGS

1 package instant soup, any flavor (Lipton preferred)
3 cups water
1 handful of spinach noodles
1 can of boneless chicken
½ onion, chopped
½ zucchini, chopped
1 jalapeño pepper, chopped
1 stalk of celery, chopped
1 pinch each of allspice, celery seed, and red pepper flakes
3 pinches curry powder

Boil the soup mix in 3 cups water. Add the noodles and chicken. While the soup is coming back to a boil, add the vegetables slowly. Stir frequently. Once all the vegetables are in and the soup has returned to a boil, turn off and cover for 5–15 minutes. Add spices and serve. This recipe can easily be improvised. It always turns out good and is reasonably healthy for you.

"I relish the simple complexities and brilliant moments of silence that only wilderness can award to the human spirit."

—Adam Washebek, Stevensville, MT

Backpackers' Smoked Salmon Marinara Tortellini
Adam Washebek, Selway–Bitterroot Wilderness

MAKES 1 SERVING

Water
3 to 5 handfuls of dried cheese-stuffed tortellini
1 tablespoon olive oil
⅛ cup dehydrated peppers
⅛ cup onion, chopped
1 packet dried marinara sauce
¼ cup dehydrated mushrooms
4–6 ounces smoked salmon (or tuna)
Tabasco Sauce to taste (optional)

In a pot with just enough water to cook the tortellini, add 3 to 5 handfuls of tortellini (depending on how hard you worked hiking), 1 tablespoon olive oil, some dehydrated peppers, chopped onion, and the packet of marinara sauce. Boil until the pasta is nearly cooked. Because mushrooms are quick to rehydrate, add them when you think you need about 3 more minutes of cook time for the tortellini. The mushrooms soak up all the excess water so there is nothing to drain. Add the smoked salmon and, if desired, some Tabasco Sauce.

"I am committed to preservation of the land. The present wilderness ethics outlined in the Wilderness Act place more muscle in the preservation of certain lands. What a great idea."

—Art Marcilla, Monte Vista, CO

Pig's Ass Chili
Art Marcilla, South San Juan Wilderness

> 1 pound diced pork
> ½ onion, chopped
> 1 tablespoon flour
> ⅓ cup water
> 1 tomato, fresh or canned, diced
> 4 ounces green chiles, fresh or canned
> Chopped garlic, salt, and pepper to taste
> ½ cup cheddar cheese (optional)

Brown the meat in a skillet, then drain out the excess grease. Add the onion and brown lightly. Add the flour and brown. Add the water, tomato, green chiles, and spices. Simmer for about 20 minutes. Spread cheese over the top of the chili, let it melt, and serve.

Leave No Trace Wilderness Tips

- Stay on designated trails.

- Avoid cutting switchbacks.

- When traveling cross-country, select routes on durable ground or through forested areas, where your tracks will not be seen.

- When traveling cross-country in a group, spread out to avoid trampling grasses and other plants.

- Leave No Trace of your visit once you're gone.

"For me, wilderness is about making deliberate choices about what's important to us as individuals and as a society."

—*Lisa Machnik, Portland, OR*

Wilderness Dinner

Lisa Machnik, Forest Service, Pacific Northwest Region

> Water (use the amount recommended by the stuffing mix plus some to
>   rehydrate the freeze-dried or dehydrated veggies)
> ¾ cup freeze-dried or dehydrated veggies, such as peas, corn, squash,
>   and spinach (or substitute fresh if early in your trip and you want to
>   carry the weight)
> ¼ cup dried cranberries
> 1½ cups premade (seasoned) whole wheat stuffing
> ¼ to ½ cup walnuts, to taste
> 1 of the following: a pouch or can of turkey or chicken, or 1 package of
>   tempeh, crumbled (optional step–toast/heat the tempeh first–not
>   necessary, but it adds a nice flavor)

Boil enough water for the stuffing (as recommended on the package), plus about ½ cup for the dried veggies. In a cup or bowl, add ½ cup boiling water to the veggies, then set aside to rehydrate/heat. Add the cranberries to the main pot of boiling water, stir, and cook for a minute or two. Add the stuffing mix, nuts, and your choice of protein. Remove from the heat and stir gently. Drain the veggies, if necessary, add to stuffing and serve! If using fresh veggies, add them to the boiling water right before adding the stuffing.

"I first prepared Cowboy Mac at White River Pass in the Bob Marshall Wilderness. The meal was filling, but the view of a feature known as the Chinese Wall inspired a lifetime commitment to preserving the open spaces that contain the wild places that we call wilderness."

—Carol Treadwell, Hungry Horse, MT

Cowboy Mac
Carol Treadwell, Bob Marshall Wilderness Foundation

MAKES 8 TO 10 SERVINGS

Water, enough to boil 2 to 3 pounds of pasta
1 onion
2 green peppers
1 red pepper
2 zucchini
1 summer squash
2 to 3 pounds bowtie pasta (multicolored is best)
1 to 2 cans black beans
3 tablespoons oil or butter
8 ounces shredded cheese, any variety
1 small container Parmesan
2 7-ounce packages tuna

Boil water for the pasta. Chop up the onion, green peppers, red pepper, zucchini, and summer squash and slightly stir-fry. Prepare the pasta as directed on the package, then drain the pasta, leaving a small amount of water in the pot. Add the veggies, black beans, and 3 tablespoons oil or butter. Heat on low for 3 to 5 minutes. Add the shredded cheese and Parmesan. Cover and let sit for 2 to 3 minutes so cheese will melt. Serve with tuna on the side, or mix the tuna into the pot (if everyone loves tuna).

Variations: Substitute cooked kielbasa or real beef hot dogs for the tuna.

"There is a special kind of comradeship in the wilderness, where we have only ourselves and our patient horses to depend on in a world without cell phones or human visitors. We look after each other in a way we never would at home. The frost on the meadow, elk in the timber, and a passing rain squall are the content of our days. The cheerful clink of hobbles in the early morning stillness starts each day. Evenings we linger around glowing aspen coals. Wilderness is special."

—Daniel Shier, Golden, CO

Corned Beef Stew
Daniel Shier, Mount Evans and Lost Creek Wildernesses

MAKES 4 SERVINGS

1 onion
1 cup freeze-dried veggies
8 ounces of pasta or quick-cook rice
Several cups of water
1 can corned beef
Black pepper to taste

Dice the onion and put in a pot. Add the veggies and pasta or rice. Add water. Simmer until tender. Add or discard water so that it just covers the cooked ingredients. Break the corned beef into small pieces and add to the pot. Bring to a boil. Add black pepper to taste.

"I grew up playing in the hardwood forests of the Midwest. Becoming a wilderness ranger seemed a logical progression of the life I loved as a child. Everyone needs to work to expand and protect our wilderness system in a truly untrammeled, pristine condition."

—*Keith Sprengel, Troutdale, OR*

Six-Grain Casserole
Keith Sprengel, Mark O. Hatfield Wilderness

MAKES 2 SERVINGS

⅛ cup bulgur wheat
⅛ cup brown rice
⅛ cup millet
⅛ cup soy grits
⅛ cup wheat berries
⅛ cup barley
Water, enough to cover grains
2 teaspoons spice mix

Combine all the grains and simmer in water for 30 minutes. Add the spice mix, combine, and serve. If you're in a deluxe camp, add cheese and veggies of your choice.

To make the spice mix: Combine equal parts curry, salt, pepper, summer savory, thyme, and garlic powder.

Selecting a Campsite

- Select a well-established campsite if you are in a popular location, or a previously unused site if you are in a remote location.

- If using an existing site, concentrate use where damage has already occurred.

- If camping in an unused site, spread out your activities. Stay off fragile plants and disperse use over a wide area.

- If in a remote location, select a site 200 feet from trails, lakes, streams, and other campsites.

"My personal wilderness philosophy is to preserve this natural/recreational resource for everyone to use and hopefully in the best, most efficient way."

—Lee Kirsch, Leadville, CO

Veggies and Pots
Lee Kirsch, Mount Massive Wilderness

1 ½ cups dried potatoes
1 ½ cups dried veggies–zucchini, bell peppers, spinach, onions, mushrooms
½ cup powdered milk
1 package instant chicken noodle soup (Lipton Cup-a-Soup preferred)
Water
Oregano, garlic powder, chili powder, and salt to taste
½ to ¾ cup grated cheddar cheese
Parmesan to taste

Put first four ingredients in a pot with enough water to cover. Cook on medium to high heat, stirring occasionally, until the potatoes and veggies are soft. Add seasonings to taste. Sprinkle with cheddar and Parmesan and serve. Fresh vegetables may be substituted for the dried ones, and in any combination desired.

"Wilderness is an escape from everyday life. It is where you can de-stress and just enjoy the beauty around you. The trees, the flowers, the grass, the rivers, lakes, animals, clouds—they all have a story to tell. By immersing yourself in their story, you can relax and forget your own worries, if only for a short moment."
—*Jenna Krebs, Lineboro, MD*

Foil Babies
Jenna Krebs, Assateague Island National Seashore (Virginia side)

> Aluminum foil
> Cooking spray or butter
> Red potatoes, cut into bite-size squares
> Bell pepper, sliced
> Zucchini, sliced
> Bacon, cooked and cut into small bits
> Shredded cheese

Take a piece of foil and form into a bowl shape. Coat the foil with cooking spray or butter. Place the potatoes and vegetables in desired proportions inside the foil bowl and fold the foil over to make a packet. Place over the coals of your campfire, occasionally stirring the contents. Depending on the size of the vegetables, cook time may vary. Once the potatoes and veggies are cooked to your liking, put bacon bits and cheese on top and allow cheese to melt before serving.

Variations: Include other types of veggies. You can also cook chunks of meat in your Foil Babies (note that cooking time will be extended). Be creative and try different ingredients in your Foil Babies. If cooking for a large group, you may want to place the veggies in an aluminum cooking tray with foil over the top to save time and room (instead of making individual packets).

"I believe wilderness should be maintained in such a way as to preserve it for future generations so that people can see what land looks like without man's influence."

—*Steve Hoots, Yampa, CO*

Flat Tops Trout
Steve Hoots, Flat Tops Wilderness

MAKES 2 TO 4 SERVINGS

4 medium-size fish, any variety
2 cups pancake batter mix
Water (amount depends on pancake batter mix)
2 tablespoons vegetable oil
Salt, pepper, and lemon pepper to taste

Catch four medium-size fish using your favorite flies or lures. Mix the pancake batter mix with water according to the directions on the package. Heat a skillet with vegetable oil (it should be hot enough to bead water). Dip the fish in the batter, then place in the skillet. Turning the fish often, cook until the batter is browned. Add seasonings to taste and serve.

Camp Stoves
Whenever possible, use a camp stove instead of building a fire. Camp stoves are more efficient for cooking, while campfires sterilize the soil and leave unsightly scars on the land.

"I became a wilderness ranger because I like the idea of having the mountains for my office, and I like working intimately with the spirit of the wilderness."
— Jan Brittain, Pollock Pines, CA

Tofu Curry
Jan Brittain, Mokelumne Wilderness

1 small bell pepper
1 small onion
2 tablespoons oil
8 ounces vacuum-packed tofu
1 package curry and shell pasta mix (if unavailable, substitute 1 cup whole wheat pasta shells, 2 tablespoons dried peas, 1 teaspoon red pepper flakes, and curry powder to taste)
1 ¼ cups water
Dried pineapple, raw coconut, raisins, and peanuts to taste

Dice the bell pepper and onion, and sauté in oil until soft. Add cubed tofu and sauté for a few more minutes. Add curry pasta mix and water. Bring to boil. Lower heat and cook for 20 minutes. Top with pineapple, coconut, raisins and peanuts and serve.

Wilderness Management

- Wilderness areas are administered for the use and enjoyment of people so long as the areas are left unimpaired for future use and enjoyment.

- Management of wilderness prohibits the use of motor vehicles, motorized equipment, and mechanical transport except in emergencies or when there is no other way to accomplish a necessary task.

- Permanent or temporary roads are not permitted.

"Our wilderness areas represent a priceless natural heritage, the last remnants of wild America in a sea of humanity and with it, 'progress' and development. The work wilderness rangers do is crucial. For without them, the wild in wilderness would be destroyed by thoughtless people."

—Eric Horstman, Weaverville, CA

Tortellini a la Trinity Alps
Eric Horstman, Trinity Alps Wilderness

MAKES 2 SERVINGS

7-ounce package tortellini
Water (enough to cover tortellini)
8 ounces tomato sauce
2 shallots, diced
4 mushrooms, diced
Cheese, oregano, salt, and pepper to taste

Add the tortellini to a pot of boiling water and cook for 10–15 minutes, until the tortellini is soft and the filling is no longer crunchy. Take the pot off the stove and drain all but a couple of teaspoons of water. Add the tomato sauce, shallots, and mushrooms, and simmer over low heat for 2–4 minutes. Season to taste with cheese, oregano, salt, and pepper.

"We all need wilderness. It's just a matter of degree. Some need broad expanses of untrammeled Alaskan landscape. For others, a flowerpot on an urban balcony may suffice. Each degree is important, and each represents a vital human connection to nature."

—*DC Carr, Sacramento, CA*

Gado-Gado Goodness
DC Carr, U.S. Fish and Wildlife Service, Pacific Southwest Region

1 tablespoon soy sauce
2 tablespoons apple cider vinegar
2 tablespoons unsalted sunflower seeds
1 tablespoon brown sugar
½ teaspoon ground cayenne
3 tablespoons vegetable oil
1 small red onion, chopped
1 bell pepper, chopped (optional)
Other chopped veggies (optional)
1 tablespoon fresh ginger, minced
3 cloves garlic, minced
½ cup natural peanut butter
4½ cups water
1½ cups uncooked fusilli pasta

To prepare at home: Combine the soy sauce and vinegar into a small, sealable container. Combine the sunflower seeds, sugar, and cayenne in a small bag. Put these, along with the other ingredients (except the water), into your bear canister.

To prepare in the field: Chop the veggies. Over the stove, heat 2 tablespoons of oil in a deep skillet or shallow saucepan. Sauté the onions until translucent, then add the remaining vegetables, ginger, and garlic. Stir to combine. Sauté about 30 seconds. Add the peanut butter and stir briefly. Quickly add ½ cup water and the vinegar/soy mixture to prevent the peanut butter from burning. Stir to combine. Add the seeds/sugar/cayenne mixture. Stir again to combine. Simmer, stirring occasionally, for about 5 minutes, or until cooked to desired consistency. Remove and cover. In a separate pot, bring the remaining 4 cups of water to a boil. Add the remaining 1 tablespoon of oil and the pasta. Simmer the pasta until tender. Drain. Combine with the sauce and serve. The sauce is tasty warm or cold.

"Wilderness is a part of the planet that is valued for itself—no strings attached. Its beauty and inaccessibility give it a quality of 'manlessness,' yet I feel comfortable being there. Mainly, I walk lightly and am there to enjoy, not destroy."

—John M. Brandon, Bozeman, MT

Pep Jack Stew

John M. Brandon, Absaroka–Beartooth Wilderness

MAKES 1 SERVING

3–4 cups water
1 handful dried veggies (onions, green peppers, tomatoes)
Dash of cooking oil
Dash of garlic powder
½ cup dried shrimp
1 cup noodles (any kind)
2 ounces of pepper jack cheese

Boil water (add more if you want soup). Add the dried veggies, oil, and garlic. Let simmer for 5 minutes. Add the dried shrimp. Add the noodles and cook until done. Drain the broth (soup in a cup) or leave it in. Grate the cheese, mix it in, and serve. It's quick, and it's spicy.

"I became a wilderness ranger because I enjoy backpacking and because I like a challenge."

—*Lisa M. Applebee, Cobalt, ID*

Chicken-Rice Curry

Lisa M. Applebee, Frank Church–River of No Return Wilderness

MAKES 1 SERVING

½ cup instant rice
¼ cup raisins
4 tablespoons margarine
4 cups water
1 package chicken noodle soup mix
2 tablespoons curry powder
1 small can of chicken

Sauté the rice and raisins in the margarine. Add the water, chicken soup mix, and curry. Bring to a boil. Simmer for 15 minutes. When the rice is almost done, stir in the chicken. Heat until the chicken is warm and serve.

"Once you have made the effort to travel into the wilderness, if nothing else, enjoy the immense beauty and the ever-changing weather."

—*Ted Scroggin, Park City, UT*

Pita Pizza
Ted Scroggin, High Uintas Wilderness

6-ounce can tomato paste
½ cup water
½–1 clove garlic
¼ teaspoon oregano
Salt and pepper to taste
4 whole mushrooms
1 handful chopped bell pepper
¼ cup chopped onion
1 scallion, chopped
2 tablespoons butter
3–4 pitas (pocket bread)
½ cup of favorite cheese, grated

Combine the tomato paste, water, garlic, oregano, salt, and pepper in a pan over medium heat. In another pan, sauté the mushrooms, bell pepper, onion, and scallion in butter for a few minutes. Combine with the sauce. In another pan, place one pita. Spread with sauce, top with cheese. Cover with a lid and heat until the cheese begins to melt. Remove and enjoy.

Campfire Tips

- Build fires only when they are legal and responsible, when conditions are safe, when there is plenty of wood, and when you have the skills to properly manage the fire.

- Build campfires away from meadows, trees, logs, and boulders.

- Keep fires small. Collect only dead or downed wood. Burn all wood in the fire pit to ashes.

- Never leave a fire unattended. Extinguish the fire by drowning it with water so that it is cold to the touch.

- Be sure to camouflage the fire site before you leave.

"Wilderness is the preservation of all that we are as animals. The air it provides fills lungs around the world, and its waters are a sweet, life-giving nectar. To be in wilderness is to be organically one and the same with belonging to nature. Wilderness is home in the purest, most intimate sense of the word."

—*Lacy Wilson, Frisco, CO*

Backcountry Sushi (Spicy Dynamite Roll)

Lacy Wilson, Carson National Forest

Rice vinegar seasoning (see below)
Instant rice
Water
Wasabi powder to taste
1 avocado
1 can shrimp, crab, salmon, or tuna
Mayonnaise packets
Dash of Sriracha (rooster sauce)
Nori (seaweed) sheets (toasted, or use a lighter to lightly toast)
Bamboo roller (nice to have, but not necessary)
Soy sauce packets

To prepare at home: Make the rice vinegar seasoning by combining 1 tablespoon rice vinegar, 3 tablespoons water, 1 teaspoon sugar, and a pinch of salt. Heat until dissolved. Mix to desired taste.

To prepare in the field: Cook equal parts rice and water for 5 minutes. Let stand. Mix a little rice vinegar seasoning with the rice. Mix the wasabi powder with very little water. Slice the avocado into long thin slices. Mix the meat, mayonnaise, and Sriracha together. Lay a nori sheet on the bamboo roller. Cover it with a layer of rice. Put a little bit of wasabi across the roll. Add the meat. Put avocado on top of the meat, and roll everything up. Cut into pieces and dip in soy sauce with wasabi.

Tip: Use rice vinegar seasoning or water on your fingers and utensils to keep the rice from sticking.

"I became a wilderness ranger because of my total fascination with the patterns of nature, whether it be leaves in the groundcover, lichens on the rock, or clouds in the sky. Benign neglect is not a wilderness management strategy."

—Judith Fraser, Cle Elum, WA

Marinated Green Beans
Judith Fraser, Alpine Lakes Wilderness

    2 cups fresh green beans
    1 small shallot, onion, or green onion, chopped
    1 clove garlic, minced
    2 tablespoons vinegar
    3 tablespoons olive oil
    1 tablespoon mixed herbs (oregano, basil, chervil, dill)
    1 tablespoon honey
    ¼ tablespoon dry mustard (optional)
    ground pepper to taste

Steam the beans until they are just tender. Then put all of the ingredients in a container and mix. A double bag, sealed baggie, or wide-mouth plastic water bottle can be used for storing beans in your pack until you're ready to eat.

"Wilderness is more than lines on a map. It is also an attitude. This attitude reflects the thought that the earth and its community of life exist for its own sake, as opposed to being for the benefit of man. Wilderness gives us the opportunity to reflect on the role of humankind as a part of the community of life, rather than as a conqueror of nature."

—*Patricia Cohn, Albuquerque, NM*

Couscous and Veggies

Patricia Cohn, Pecos Wilderness

MAKES 2 CUPS

1 ¼ cups water
½ cup dried veggies (any kind)
½ cup couscous
Vegetable broth, lemon, ramen seasoning to taste

Boil the water. Add the dried veggies and cook for 2 or 3 minutes. Add the couscous and remove from heat. Cover and let sit for 5 minutes. Add seasonings and serve. You can also use fresh vegetables, but it takes longer to cook.

"My parents, grandparents, and uncle instilled in me a great love and respect for the land. The feeling of happiness and peace of mind that comes from the beauty of nature is so very precious. We need to protect our wilderness."

—*Janice Chapman, Gunnison, CO*

Dad's Surprise
Janice Chapman, La Garita Wilderness

MAKES 2–4 SERVINGS

1 small red onion, diced
3 small yellow summer squash, sliced
1 green pepper, diced
1 tablespoon oil
2 small cans spicy-hot V8 Juice
1 cup water
1 package dried Spanish rice
1 cup shredded mozzarella

Add the veggies to the heated oil in a pan and cover loosely with a lid. Stir often for about 5 minutes, then set aside. In a different pan, combine the V8 Juice, water, and rice and bring to a boil. Let simmer for about 15 minutes without a lid. Add the veggies into the rice and stir. Sprinkle cheese on top and cover until melted. Serve.

The Life of a Wilderness Ranger

The life of a wilderness ranger is not your typical 9-to-5 job. It's not about dress clothes or boardrooms. Nor are you tethered to a desk, a phone, or a computer.

It's a life filled with adventure and discovery. There's also the humbling realization that nature—in all its glory—is totally in charge. You are only a visitor to the great American landscapes designated by Congress as wilderness.

The hours are long. You are often up before dawn preparing a tried-and-true breakfast on a one-burner stove (perhaps one of the recipes found in this cookbook). Once the sun breaks over the horizon, you pack up for the trail.

Your assignment for the day might be cleaning water bars so the rains won't wash out the switchbacks you built last season. Or you might be collecting native seeds to replant at a camp spot that has lost its ground-cover to thousands of footprints. Maybe you'll come across some visitors along the trail. You'll share how to enjoy these fragile landscapes without causing harm.

Depending on the wilderness you work in, you may not see another living soul for days. You must be willing to camp, hike, ride horseback, pack a mule, lead llamas, row a raft, or paddle a canoe or kayak on your own. You must relish the oneness of it all. You must feel totally comfortable in the vastness of the outdoors and confident that you can handle the elements: thunderstorms, mosquitoes, chiggers, black flies, snakes, and the howling wind. You must be backcountry-smart, using all of your senses to taste the air, smell the danger, and know when to stop.

As a wilderness ranger, you are master of a thousand skills, from orienteering to operating a crosscut saw (chain saws are prohibited unless under certain circumstances). You are a naturalist, an interpreter, and a researcher. You are a cloud observer and stargazer. You are a member of the search-and-rescue team.

You do it all, and you do it with a love for the land and all things wild and free. The best rangers retain a childlike wonder of the awesomeness of nature. While on patrol, you constantly ask: What's over that mountain pass? Where does this waterway lead? Only when you know your wilderness like the back of your hand are equipped for the job of being a ranger.

Yes, you serve the public, and you do it with pride, dignity, and honor. But you also serve a higher order. You serve the wholeness of wild lands, trying your best to not allow yourself or others to take the wild out of wilderness.

To be a wilderness ranger is to live the life you dreamed about. The land needs dedicated wilderness rangers to watch over it. And those best suited for the job find that they need wilderness too. Only when they get lost in wilderness do they truly find themselves.

"Wilderness cannot be underused, only overused."

—Charlie Hellen, Tollhouse, CA

Chicken-Chuck
Charlie Hellen, John Muir Wilderness

MAKES 3 SERVINGS

3 boneless chicken breasts, halved
1 tablespoon olive oil
8-ounce can pineapple chunks
1 large red onion
1 large green sweet pepper
1 large red sweet pepper
2 ounces apple juice
Water, per directions on rice
1 cup instant rice

In a large skillet, brown lightly both sides of the chicken breasts in olive oil. Add the pineapple juice and chunks. Ring cut the onion and peppers. Add the vegetables to the skillet, along with apple juice. Cover and simmer over medium heat for 20 minutes. Meanwhile, boil amount of water needed for instant rice. Add the rice, turn down the heat, and let it simmer until the rice is soft. Serve the chicken over a bed of rice.

Memorable Words on Wilderness

"We abuse the land because we regard it as a commodity belonging to us. When we see land as a community to which we belong, we may begin to use it with love and respect."

—Aldo Leopold, wilderness leader

"Teaching people to love and respect wilderness instills hope for future generations. If today's children find the importance in wilderness, then tomorrow's children will have a chance to discover that magic as well. Through education and exploration we can help facilitate this journey for youth, and that can be a powerful thing to be a part of."

—Katelyn Rennicke, Juneau, AK

Curry in a Hurry

Katelyn Rennicke, Tracy Arm–Fords Terror Wilderness Crew

Water
½ package Asian rice noodles
1 package dried mushrooms, any variety
1 red pepper, chopped
1 yellow squash, chopped
⅓ yellow onion, chopped
3 cloves garlic, chopped
1 inch chunk ginger, chopped
1 can coconut milk
½ pack of red curry paste
Fish sauce and Bragg Liquid Aminos to taste
½ lime
⅓ bunch cilantro, chopped

Boil water for the rice noodles and dried mushrooms using amount of water called for in package directions. Let both soak for 20 minutes. In another pot, mix the chopped pepper, squash, onion, garlic, and ginger with the coconut milk. Bring to a boil, then simmer for about 10 minutes. Add the noodles and mushrooms to the veggie/coconut mix and stir. Add the red curry paste (consider your field partners' tolerance for spicy food) and stir well. Add fish sauce and Bragg Liquid Aminos to taste. Squeeze the lime and sprinkle the cilantro on individual servings.

"The opportunity to work in a wilderness setting and to make a difference in the effort to preserve wilderness is an unbeatable combination."

—Rob Bleiberg, Dillon, CO

Alpine Tortellini with Pesto Sauce
Rob Bleiberg, Eagles Nest Wilderness

MAKES 2 TO 3 SERVINGS

Water
8- or 10-ounce package of tortellini (make sure you get the kind that doesn't need to be refrigerated)
2 tablespoons butter
1 packet instant pesto sauce
1 ounce pine nuts or unsalted cashews
½ ounce Parmesan

Bring a pot of water to a boil. Add the tortellini, reduce the heat, and cover. When the tortellini is soft, leave it covered and set it aside. In another pan, melt the butter and add the pesto sauce (use the instructions on the pesto sauce package). Drain the tortellini and add the pesto sauce and nuts. Sprinkle with Parmesan and serve.

Leave No Trace Wilderness Tips

- Trenching around your tent is unnecessary.

- Stay only one night in any one campsite to minimize impact.

- If camping for several days at an undisturbed site, move your tent every day.

- Avoid building camp structures.

- Wash dishes, clothes, and yourself 200 feet from any stream or lake.

- Pour strained wash water in a sump hole or broadcast it widely.

- Cover catholes, latrines, and sump holes thoroughly before breaking camp.

- Pick up every bit of trash and food and pack it out.

"I chose to be a wilderness ranger to get back to the mountains I love."
—Nate Inouye, Steamboat Springs, CO

Ginger Desperation over Rice
Nate Inouye, Mount Zirkel Wilderness

MAKES 2 HEARTY SERVINGS

1 cup rice
2 cups water
½ pound hamburger
2 tablespoons grated gingerroot
1 cup chopped broccoli
1 cup chopped cauliflower
½ lemon
Honey to taste
Soy sauce to taste

Rinse rice and put it in a covered pot with water. Bring to a boil at high heat. Turn the stove down and simmer the rice until done (20–40 minutes depending on stove and altitude). Brown the hamburger in a large, covered pot over medium heat. Drain the excess grease. Add the gingerroot, broccoli, and cauliflower, and simmer over low heat 5–10 minutes (the vegetables should remain crisp). Squeeze lemon over the veggies and meat and mix. Add honey and soy sauce to taste. Serve over hot rice.

"Wilderness—land we have set aside to protect for future and current generations so all can experience what true wild is . . . "

—Triston Richardson, Pagosa Springs, CO

Landlocked Gumbo
Triston Richardson, South San Juan Wilderness

MAKES 2 SERVINGS

1 box of red beans and rice mix
1 6- to 8-ounce can of organic chicken
1 4-ounce can diced green chiles
8 ounces Monterey Jack cheese, sliced
2 flour tortillas
1 avocado

Make the red beans and rice as instructed on the box. With 5 minutes remaining on the cook time, place the chicken, green chiles with juice, and sliced cheese in with the beans and rice. Let the pot sit for 5 minutes, or until the beans and rice thicken. Serve with tortillas and sliced avocado.

"My personal wilderness philosophy is that all land managers should have their first trainings in wilderness."

—Walter Werner, Aspen, CO

Snowmass Trout
Walter Werner, Maroon Bells–Snowmass Wilderness

MAKES 4 SERVINGS

⅓ cup cornmeal
⅓ cup baking mix (such as Bisquick) or plain flour
½ teaspoon cornstarch
Black pepper to taste
4 legally caught trout
10 slices bacon
10 ounces stuffed green olives
2 cloves garlic

Mix cornmeal, baking mix, cornstarch, and pepper. Catch and clean four 8- to 10-inch trout (release any trout over 12 inches). Fry the bacon until chewy. Remove the bacon from the pan and set aside. Heat the green olives in the bacon grease. Slice the garlic and place equal amounts in the body cavities of the fish. Roll the fish in cornmeal mixture. Slice the chewy bacon into two-inch strips and wrap it around the olives, then fry until the bacon is crisper. Remove the wrapped olives from the pan and fry the fish until golden brown. While frying the fish, enjoy the wrapped olives as hors d'oeuvres.

"The value of wilderness increases daily. To walk in wild landscapes is a powerful force, one that calls us back and makes us marvel at the wonder of it all."
—Ralph Swain, Evergreen, CO

Burrito Power
Ralph Swain, Forest Service, Rocky Mountain Region

MAKES 4 SERVINGS

8-ounce can refried beans
2 whole jalapeño peppers (the hotter, the better)
6-ounce can whole kernel corn
3-ounce can diced black olives
1 package whole wheat tortillas
Grated swiss cheese to taste
3 ounces yogurt or sour cream
3 ounces salsa

Combine the beans, sliced peppers, corn, and olives in a pan. Cook until warm. Remove from the heat and cover. In a skillet, warm the tortillas. Spread some bean mixture onto a tortilla. Sprinkle with cheese. Fold the tortilla over and heat until cheese melts. Top with yogurt or sour cream and salsa. Serve. Continue the assembly process until everyone screams enough!

Hint: Put the first four ingredients in a container the night before to let the flavors blend.

Be Considerate of Others

- Keep pets under control at all times. If possible, leave them at home.

- Keep noise at acceptable levels while hiking or camping. Loud noises can spook wildlife and diminish others' solitude.

"Wilderness provides me with mental, physical, and spiritual healing, but overuse and overcrowding are threatening that. I think we should put much more emphasis on preservation and less on providing recreation."

—*Sharon Napp, Skykomish, WA*

Red Lentil Glop
Sharon Napp, Henry M. Jackson Wilderness

MAKES 1 SERVING

Water
2 small handfuls red lentils
1 small handful sunflower seeds
1 or 2 handfuls dried onions, mushrooms, and zucchini
Pepper, garlic powder, cayenne pepper, and onion powder to taste
1 to 2 ounces cheese, cut in small chunks, any variety

Bring the water to a boil. Add all ingredients except cheese (if using fresh veggies, add them after 5 minutes). Boil until the lentils are reasonably soft– 6–8 minutes. Remove from heat. Pour out excess water. Add the cheese and stir until melted. Shovel into your mouth with a trusty spoon.

"Wilderness, both protected and unprotected, offers us a chance to connect with our environment as an equal among its features and inhabitants. I think it's becoming increasingly rare to have those experiences in a world where we so casually rely on our technology and so frequently alter our physical environment. It is a nourishing treat to experience the world in such pure symbiosis."

—Ryan Stolp, Durham, NC

Joe Dirtay Pancake Pizza
Ryan Stolp, Linville Gorge Wilderness

MAKES 2 8-INCH PIZZAS

1 ½ cups pancake mix
1 cup flour
Water
Oregano to taste
1 small can tomato paste or dehydrated tomato paste
1 packet spaghetti seasoning
4 to 6 ounces cheese, grated
Vegetable or meat toppings of choice

Mix the pancake mix and flour with water until evenly mixed (your spoon should leave a short trail). Season with oregano. Pour a big pancake into a frying pan on low heat. When the edges of the crust begin to cook, flip. Spread a thin layer of tomato paste on the pancake and season with the spaghetti mix. Top with cheese and toppings. To melt the cheese faster, sprinkle the pan with water and cover with a lid. Cook until the cheese is melted, then serve.

"I learned how to live off the land when I was young, and I had a sense of my own wilderness ethic long before anyone taught me what I know and practice today."
—*Rich Hamilton, Creede, CO*

Mountain Brook Trout
Rich Hamilton, Weminuche Wilderness

MAKES 1 SERVING

1 brook trout
2 tablespoons butter
1 teaspoon lemon juice
1 teaspoon garlic (or more to taste)
½ teaspoon dill weed
3 bacon strips

Catch a cunning mountain brook trout. (I recommend using a ⅛-ounce Panther Martin spinning lure or a black nymph fly, a light test line, and a sneaky upstream approach.) Once the fish is caught and cleaned, prepare two sheets of foil large enough to seal the catch. Add all ingredients and seal the foil packet tightly. The bacon fat keeps the fish from burning. Cook over medium-high heat, turning the packet every few minutes, until it's sizzling (about 20 minutes). Serve.

"Wilderness is a great teacher of living systems—present, past, and future—and an outstanding place for personal re-creation and recreation. It demands our care and our respect."

—Lois Ziemann, Jackson, WY

Tortellini with Clams
Lois Ziemann, Gros Ventre Wilderness

MAKES 2 SERVINGS

8-ounce package of tortellini
Water, enough to cover tortellini plus extra to add to milk powder
3 tablespoons hard butter
1 small can clams
1 cup nonfat dry milk powder mixed with enough water to make it thick
¼ cup chopped green pepper
¼ cup chopped red pepper
½ cup chopped mushrooms
1 chopped red onion (optional)
Parmesan
Italian seasoning to taste (mix equal parts oregano, basil, garlic salt,
        coarse black pepper, and add a pinch of thyme)

Boil the tortellini in water until done. Drain off the water. Add the butter. When melted, add the other ingredients and cook until heated through. (Note: If you don't like your veggies crunchy, boil them along with the tortellini.)

Memorable Words on Wilderness

"We don't inherit the earth from our ancestors; we borrow it from our children."

—Unknown

"Wilderness rangers have the challenging opportunity to encourage the public to participate in preserving wildlands. All wilderness visitors must learn to adjust their needs to nature, rather than adjusting nature to their needs."

—Tracey McInerney, Durango, CO

Alpine Spaghetti

Tracey McInerney, Weminuche Wilderness

MAKES 1 SERVING

1 handful spaghetti noodles
4 or 5 cups of water
1 tablespoon olive oil or safflower oil
½ cup pinon nuts
½ cup grated Romano
¼ cup raisins
½ tablespoon Italian seasoning (equal parts basil, thyme, oregano, and garlic powder)

Add the spaghetti to boiling water. Mix in the oil. Cook until the pasta is soft. Drain the water and add the rest of the ingredients. Heat until warm. This is delicious served with wild greens or an alfalfa sprout salad.

"If we really want to save what is left of the wilderness, aren't we really trying to save ourselves?"

—Hal Wentz, Walden, CO

Backcountry Burritos
Hal Wentz, Mount Zirkel Wilderness

MAKES 10–12 SERVINGS

2 cups water
1 package dried refried beans
Hard cheese, 6 to 8 ounces
Hot sauce to taste
1 head of lettuce, shredded
1 tomato, diced
10–12 tortillas

Bring 2 cups of water to boil. Add the dehydrated beans. Stir occasionally, and let stand 5 minutes. Put the beans, cheese, hot sauce, lettuce, and tomatoes on the tortillas and eat.

Packing with Animals

- Take the minimum number of animals needed.

- During short stops, use crossties attached between two trees that are at least 8 inches in diameter to contain stock animals. Avoid picketing pack animals. If you must picket, move the pickets frequently.

- Keep tied, picketed, and hobbled pack animals well away from trails, camps, lakes, and streams.

- Tie, picket, or hobble animals only in dry areas, preferably on hard, dry ground, to minimize trampling damage to vegetation.

- When meeting stock users on a trip, hikers and backpackers should step off the lower side of the trail and stand still while the riders pass.

"Wilderness is the most important thing our country has. We need to designate more as soon as possible so future generations will be able to experience nature at her finest. We must never forget that at one time our whole country was wilderness. Look what's available after only 200 years."

—Gregg Heid, Aurora, CO

Taco Salad
Gregg Heid, Indian Peaks Wilderness

1 15-ounce can chili con carne
3 ounces mild or hot salsa
1 or 2 handfuls of tortilla chips
½ tomato
½ small onion
¼ head of lettuce
2 to 3 ounces grated cheddar cheese

Heat up the chili and salsa in a saucepan. Pour over a plate of crushed tortilla chips (easily prepared by putting the bag in the bottom of your backpack). Dice up the tomato, onion, and lettuce. Mix with the chips and chili. Cover with grated cheese. Let the cheese melt and enjoy.

"To me, wilderness is as close as we can come to time travel. Losing the sights and sounds of everyday urban life and coming back into the ancient cadences of being outside, which our bodies understand but our brains have temporarily forgotten, is an essential and magical journey."

—*Jay A. Satz, Seattle, WA*

Lucchetti's Backcountry Clam Linguini
Jay A. Satz, Yellowstone National Park

MAKES 4 SERVINGS

1¼ cups extra virgin olive oil
1 small onion, thinly sliced
1 small red pepper, thinly sliced
2 6.5-ounce cans of clams, preferably whole (if cooking at home, use one
     can clams and 1 pound fresh clams in the shell steamed in ½ cup
     water)
¼ cup white wine
Fresh ground pepper and salt to taste
Rosemary, oregano, or thyme to taste
Linguine or your favorite pasta, cooked according to package directions

Heat half the olive oil in a frying pan and sauté the onions and red peppers until the onions are translucent, about 10 minutes. Add the clams and accompanying liquid from the can (if using fresh clams, also add ¼ cup of the steaming water). Cook vigorously for about five minutes, then add the remaining olive oil, wine, and spices. Simmer the sauce for 15 minutes. Serve over the pasta of choice.

"Being out in the wilderness is a wonderful contrast to my life in Cincinnati. Each lifestyle helps me to appreciate the other more. By working hard, eating well, and laughing at frequent and regular intervals, you and the wilderness will take care of each other."

—*Julia Becker, Ennis, MT*

Regurgitate de la Prospector con Yama Yama
Julia Becker, Lee Metcalf Wilderness

Water
1 cup rice
½ cup lentils
15 prunes, pitted
1 handful sunflower seeds
½ handful flax seeds
1 tea bag barley tea
1 heaping tablespoon margarine
1 handful seaweed
Dash of cayenne (if you like it hot)
2 dashes each lemon thyme, dill, basil, and sage
5–6 large slices of cheese (your favorite)

In a saucepan with water, cook up the rice with the lentils, prunes, and seeds. Once boiling, dip the tea bag in the cooking water for 5–10 minutes. Then add the margarine, seaweed, cayenne, and spices. Mix. When the rice mixture is nearly done, add the cheese, reduce the heat, and cover the pot until the cheese is melted. Drive a spoon through the crust and gorge.

"Wilderness is a state of mind where you can get back to the basics of life itself, a place to re-evaluate what is important in life, to test values, and to discover new facets within yourself. If wilderness should ever disappear, the human race will have forever lost its ability to discover life as it has evolved and implications for life in the future."

—*Karen L. Kromrey, Moose Pass, AK*

Chicken Ramen Goulash
Karen L. Kromrey, Rawah Wilderness

MAKES 2 SERVINGS

1 package chicken ramen noodles
6½ ounces of canned chicken
Fresh sliced mushrooms (as many as you want)
½ cup chopped celery
Other vegetables (optional)
Salt and pepper to taste

Make the ramen soup according to the directions on the package. Just before the noodles are cooked, add the remaining ingredients. Heat the soup until the chicken and veggies are warm, then serve.

Climate Change and Wilderness

- Water: Climate change is predicted to increase drought risk and severity, decrease snowpack, and reduce summer river and stream flows. In the western states, more than 50 percent of the water supply comes from wilderness areas, and this clean, fresh water is vital to wilderness and to the American people.

- Fire: Warmer temperatures from longer growing seasons will increase the risk of more numerous and severe forest fires. Allowing wildfires to burn in some wilderness areas over the last 40 years has been shown to reduce the likelihood and intensity of future fires. The lessons can be applied across all lands to deal with altered fire regimes under a rapidly warming climate.

- Plants and animals: Some plant and animal species are at risk of extinction as temperatures and precipitation patterns change. Some species will migrate to new habitats—and wilderness areas will provide important migration corridors and refuges for biodiversity.

- Research: Large, undisturbed wilderness landscapes serve as natural laboratories and benchmarks for monitoring the impacts of climate variability now and climate change in the future.

- Society: Wilderness is defined in the Wilderness Act as an area of undeveloped federal land "where the earth and its community of life are untrammeled by man" (section 2c). Untrammeled means unhindered or not subject to human control. Wilderness is self-willed and defined by restraint—societal restraint and individual restraint. Leaving wilderness untrammeled, with minimum human influence and intervention, will test future wilderness managers and scientists.

"I believe it is up to each individual to do whatever he can to preserve our natural environment."

—*Steve Comeaux, Russellville, AR*

Cajun-Style Fish and Rice
Steve Comeaux, Dry Creek Wilderness

MAKES 3 SERVINGS

4 cups white rice
Water, per directions for rice plus ½ cup
1 large onion
2–3 cloves garlic
4 ounces butter
1 cup dry white wine (optional)
1 teaspoon salt
1 tablespoon red pepper flakes
3 tablespoons black pepper
16 ounces fish fillets

Cook the rice in water per package directions. Dice the onion and garlic and brown in butter over medium heat for 10 minutes. Add ½ cup water (or wine) and the seasonings to the onion and garlic mixture. Cover and simmer on low heat for 30 minutes, stirring occasionally. Add the fish, cover, and simmer for an additional 10 minutes. Don't overcook. Serve the fish over the rice.

"Some of my fondest memories growing up are of wild areas that my father took me to and worked in. I would like to see future generations enjoy the benefits of seeing these wild areas in their original, pristine states. Through education and preservation, we can assure the areas stay that way."

—*Scott Edwards, Creede, CO*

Ute Lake Tacos
Scott Edwards, Weminuche Wilderness

MAKES 3 TO 4 SERVINGS

½–1 pound ground beef
Cumin, garlic, and chili powder to taste
1–2 tablespoons cooking oil
6 blue corn tortillas
4 green onions, chopped
1 cup sharp cheddar cheese
Grated salsa to taste

Cook the ground beef in a skillet. Add the seasonings. Pour the oil into a separate small pan and heat. Fill each tortilla with beef, onions, and cheese. Fold over into a sandwich. Fry both sides for about 1 minute. Remove from the pan. Drain on paper towel or cloth. Add salsa to taste and serve.

Note: The ground beef can also be cooked at home and sealed in an airtight container. It will last for about 5 days.

Variation: Add diced cooked potatoes to the meat mixture.

"Wilderness, and the defense of it, has been the focus of my professional career, but it is also the soul-calming solace that makes even the most desperate times seem small, manageable, and short-lived. It is the calming of one's mind. It is the restoration of one's soul."

— Lisa Hendy, Yosemite, CA

Tuckup Canyon Tortellini

Lisa Hendy, Yosemite National Park

MAKES 1 SERVING

Assorted chopped veggies (I like broccoli and grape tomatoes)
1 teaspoon Parmesan, shredded
1 tablespoon pesto
Water (enough to cover pasta)
1 cup dry tortellini
1 tablespoon pine nuts or shredded almonds
Pinch of salt

To prepare at home: Chop the veggies before you leave and throw the Parmesan in with them in a sealed baggie. I store the pesto in tiny plastic jars for transport.

To prepare in the field: Boil water and add the pasta. When the tortellini are done, drain until just a tablespoon or so of water is left, then throw in the veggies and Parmesan. Stir frequently and cook down the last of the water. Add pesto, nuts, and salt. Enjoy!

Variation: Add chicken. Use canned if that appeals to you; I pack in strips of the frozen precooked chicken. The chicken thaws by dinnertime, and I add it to the dish at the same time as the veggies.

"Americans should be proud that they have created huge swaths of wilderness in the U.S., which contribute immensely to preserving biodiversity and the global environment on which all life depends. Next, each American can take actions that provide sustainable stewardship for the continuity of its preservation."

—*Michael Olwyler, North Fork, CA*

Simple Mountain Bulgur
Michael Olwyler, Ansel Adams Wilderness

½ package minestrone soup mix (Knorr preferred)
2⅓ cups water
1 cup bulgur wheat
1 clove garlic, smashed
1 small zucchini, chopped
1 small carrot, chopped
1 small can chicken in water (optional)

Combine the soup mix with the water and bring to a boil. Pour in the bulgur wheat and add the garlic. Stir. Bring the mixture back to a boil. Turn the stove down to low, cover the pot, and let the bulgur cook for 12 minutes. Check to ensure that it doesn't burn. Add the veggies and chicken, and cook for another 4–5 minutes until done. Add more water as needed. The more variety of veggies you add, the more tasty the recipe.

"Doing my part has been a personal commitment for me. Hopefully the people I meet in my classes and as a ranger will learn no-trace skills. If these people go away caring more deeply about the wilderness and its future, I have done my job."
— *Barbara Hartman, Buffalo, WY*

Whole Grain Baking Mix
Barbara Hartman, Cloud Peak Wilderness

MAKES 6 BISCUITS OR 1 PIZZA

2 cups all-purpose flour
2 cups whole wheat flour
¾ cup dry milk powder
½ cup quick oats
½ cup cornmeal
2 tablespoons baking powder
1 teaspoon salt
1 cup shortening

Pizza
½ package of active dry yeast
1 cup baking mix
4 ounces pizza sauce
Grated cheese, as desired

To prepare at home: In a large container, thoroughly combine the dry ingredients. Using a pastry blender, mix in the shortening until evenly dispersed. Store tightly covered for up to 2 weeks at room temperature, or up to several months in the refrigerator.

To prepare in the field: For whole grain biscuits, use 1 cup mix and ⅓ cup water. Mix just until moistened. Drop dough by spoonfuls on a greased skillet, cover, and cook 10–12 minutes.

For whole-grain-crust pizza: Soften ½ package of active dry yeast in ¼ cup warm water. Stir in 1 cup baking mix. Knead 25 strokes, then let rest 10 minutes. Grease a skillet. Pat the crust onto bottom of pan, building up edges. Cook 10 minutes. Spread 4 ounces pizza sauce on the crust, then sprinkle with desired toppers. Top with cheese. Cook 10 minutes or until cheese is melted. **Hint:** Put a heat diffuser between the skillet and flame to keep the bottom from overcooking.

"Let us all work together to protect this fragile environment so posterity, too, may gaze on the borders of beauty herself."

—*Koji Kawamura, Aspen, CO*

Upside Down Pizza
Koji Kawamura, Maroon Bells–Snowmass Wilderness

MAKES 1 PIZZA

1 teaspoon sugar
Dash of salt
1 tablespoon oil
1 cup lukewarm water
1 tablespoon yeast
2½ cups flour
1 pound mozzarella, grated
1 cup mushrooms, sliced
1 cup tomato sauce

Dissolve the sugar, salt, and oil in lukewarm water (100°F). Dissolve the yeast into the water solution. Let stand 5 minutes. Combine the yeast mixture with flour until the dough is not sticky, and knead well. Let the dough rise about 15 minutes. Flatten the dough and cook it in a skillet over a low flame. Turn the dough over and cook the other side until light brown. Set aside. In the skillet, add the cheese and mushrooms, or any other pizza toppings. Add the tomato sauce. Place the crust on top of the sauce. Cook to 10 minutes on a low flame or until the cheese browns. Flip the pie over and let stand for a few minutes before serving.

Variation: Use a packet of spaghetti sauce mix with tomato paste instead of tomato sauce.

"After spending thirty years working in natural resource management, I realize how lucky I was to start out as a wilderness ranger. The Rawahs provided a solid foundation for my career, and the National Wilderness Preservation System provides a solid foundation for all natural resource conservation in North America."
—Kenneth M. Brink Jr., Roxborough, CO

Veggie Spaghetti
Kenneth M. Brink Jr., Rawah Wilderness

MAKES 2 SERVINGS

1 small zucchini
1 small onion
2 packages ramen noodles
Water
1 teaspoon Italian herbs
½ teaspoon garlic powder
1 small can tomato paste

Start by thinly slicing the zucchini and thinly chopping the onion. Boil the noodles and zucchini together in water until cooked. Drain all but about ½ cup of the water and add the spices, tomato paste, and onions. Stir and heat as desired.

Walk softly on the land . . . Leave No Trace. Visit www.LNT.org for ready-made lesson plans for protecting and preserving wilderness. *Courtesy Leave No Trace Center for Outdoor Ethics*

"As humans, we have created anthropocentric rights; it took little time to learn how to abuse those rights in relation to wilderness. Wilderness, the natural occurring ecosystems, is like earth's child—innocent and naive."

—*S. Bud Solmonsson, Kemah, TX*

Quesa Noché (Cheese Night)
S. Bud Solmonsson, Trinity Alps Wilderness

MAKES 3 TO 6 SERVINGS

3–6 flour tortillas
1 onion, chopped
1 bell pepper, chopped
Salsa to taste (optional)
½ pound cheese of choice

Cook a tortilla over medium heat in a pan. Sprinkle chopped onions, bell peppers, and salsa over one half of the tortilla while it is cooking. Then put cheese over the same half, on top of the other ingredients. As soon as cheese starts to melt, fold the untouched tortilla half over to make a half circle. Turn the quesa noché over, heat until all the cheese is melted, and serve.

Note: If served for lunch or breakfast, this will not be a quesa noché, but rather a quesa dia (cheese day).

"Wilderness is our future. Without such places, we could never have serenity, peace within ourselves, or dreams. We need to properly preserve such places so future generations will have a chance to experience them. Can you imagine a world without the beauty and magic of wilderness? What would we daydream about?"

—*Lise Hall, Carbondale, CO*

Crab and Cheese Curry
Lise Hall, Flat Tops Wilderness

MAKES 2 SERVINGS

⅓ cup powdered milk
1–2 cups water
¼ cup rice
1½ tablespoons butter
1½ tablespoons flour
1½ teaspoons curry powder
Dash of salt
2 dashes of pepper
4 ounces cheese, any variety, grated
4 ounces crab flakes

Mix the powdered milk and 1 cup water. Set aside. Cook the rice with water per the package directions and set aside. Melt the butter in a medium pan. Stir in the flour to create a paste. Slowly stir in the milk. Heat for a few minutes, then add the spices and cheese. When the cheese has partially melted, stir in the crab flakes. (Keep the crab flakes frozen until you are ready to leave for your trip; they will last 2 or 3 days.) Heat the crab until hot. Serve over rice.

Wilderness Fact

More than 32,500 acres in Michigan was designated as the Sleeping Bear Dunes Wilderness on March 13, 2014, making it the first congressional wilderness designation since 2009.

"The wilderness is very fragile, and we must manage it closely. Some say, 'Leave it alone. It will take care of itself.' This may have been true years ago when the use was minimal, but today, the wilderness is taking a beating. It must be managed for future generations to enjoy so they can say, 'I'm in the wilderness, an unspoiled area unlike any other on earth.'"

—*Greg Marks, Shaver Lake, CA*

Coyote Lake Zucchini
Greg Marks, John Muir Wilderness

> 2 zucchini
> 1 small can tomato sauce (substitute 1 package of tomato soup mix if desired)
> 1 package onion soup mix
> Water
> 1 ½ cups instant rice
> 1 cup grated cheese (use your favorite)

Slice the zucchini and place in a pot with the tomato sauce. Mix in the onion soup mix and ½ cup water. Let this simmer at low heat until the zucchini are tender. In another pot, prepare the instant rice according to its directions. Once the zucchini is tender and the rice is done, mix the ingredients of the two pots together. Add grated cheese, mix evenly, and chow down.

How Much Should Your Pack Weigh?

- As a rule of thumb, pack weight should not be more than one third of your body weight.

- Your food weight should not be more than one fourth of your pack weight.

"Wilderness feeds and restores the soul, the body, and the mind. It is unique, fragile, and ever-changing, just like those of us who visit and the wild creatures who call it home."

—*Terry Carlson, Missoula, MT*

Chicken and Dumplings
Terry Carlson, Comanche Peak Wilderness

MAKES 2 SERVINGS

1 cup flour
2 teaspoons baking powder
¼ cup powdered milk
Salt to taste
4½ cups water
2 tablespoons vegetable oil
1 small can or package of chicken
1 celery stalk, chopped
1 carrot, chopped
½ onion, chopped
Thyme, oregano, basil, pepper, parsley, and sage to taste

Dumplings: Mix the flour, baking powder, milk, and salt together. Add ½ cup of water and the oil, then mix until the dry ingredients are moistened.

Chicken broth: Combine the chicken, celery, carrot, onion, and spices with 4 cups of water in a pot. Bring to a boil. Reduce the heat. Drop the dumpling dough by spoonfuls into the broth. Cover tightly and simmer for about 15 minutes (try not to lift the lid) until the dumplings are cooked.

Variations: Add zucchini, chili powder, green chiles, or cabbage to the chicken broth. Substitute ramen or veggie noodles for the dumplings.

"Wilderness is a place we can escape the clutter, fast pace, and complex life of society, where we can lose touch with our 'self' and reconnect to the natural, wild, and free world because true wilderness doesn't show the sign of man . . . only the Great Outdoors."

—*Dustan Hoffman, Seney, MI*

Spring Harvest Salad
Dustan Hoffman, Seney National Wildlife Refuge

> Watercress (leaves and stems, raw)
> Wild leek (leafy greens, raw)
> Dandelion greens (young, raw)
> Trout lily leaves
> Wild asparagus (raw)
> Fiddleheads (sautéed)
> Wild leek (bulb, sautéed)
> Wild gingerroot (minced and mixed with olive oil and rice vinegar to taste for a dressing)

Gathering different greens in the spring months can yield a tasty addition to any meal. This recipe is free for interpretation with types of greens and amounts because you never know what edibles you'll find when foraging for food, and there are no guarantees on how much of an edible you will find. Use several different field guides to help you identify plants until you are confident in the plants you are harvesting. Be sure you aren't harvesting any lookalike species. In unfamiliar areas, it may be necessary to consult more guides to make sure you are choosing edibles.

Sautéing the greens should be done in the way that suits the cook. My personal preference is to sauté greens together—after all, they will be tasted in the same bite and cookware is in short supply in the backcountry. To prepare, just mix together what you've harvested and enjoy.

"I like the feel of clean air making its way into and out of my body. The idea of preserving and protecting the wildness, including the air resource of certain areas, appeals to me. I support the wilderness concept to ensure that I, my children, and your children can breathe free at any cost."

—*Karl F. Zeller, Wellington, CO*

Dandelion Salad
Karl F. Zeller, Cache La Poudre Wilderness

MAKES 1 SERVING

4 slices bacon
2 tablespoons vinegar
1 tablespoon lemon juice (optional)
2 tablespoons brown sugar
¼ teaspoon salt
6 cups young, tender dandelion leaves
1 hard-boiled egg (optional)

Cook the bacon. When done, remove and cool the grease. Add vinegar, lemon juice, sugar, and salt to the bacon grease and heat slowly while stirring. Pour the hot bacon dressing over the washed and dried dandelion greens. Add the chopped egg and crumbled bacon on top and eat as you watch the clouds roll by.

Variation: Add 2 tablespoons sour cream and 1 beaten raw egg to the grease before reheating.

Dandelions

The young leaves of this familiar weed are good in soups and salads. The older leaves need cooking—and butter, salt, and pepper. Wine is made from the heads of the plant.

Roxana Bashyrova/Shutterstock

"We need to consider ourselves renters, not owners, of the land, and care for it as if we would be tolled for any damages we may have done."
—*Barbara Walker, Kamas, UT*

Linguini and Clams
Barbara Walker, High Uintas Wilderness

> 1 tablespoon dried onion
> ½ cup dried mushrooms
> Water
> ½ cup olive oil
> ½ teaspoon pepper
> 1 teaspoon dried oregano
> 2 tablespoons dried basil
> 3 cloves garlic (or 1 teaspoon dried garlic)
> 3 tablespoons dried parsley
> 6-ounce can clams
> 16 ounces linguini noodles
> ½ cup Parmesan

Reconstitute the onions and mushrooms in water for a few minutes. Drain. Sauté onions and mushrooms in oil. Add herbs and seasonings. Pour in the juice from the can of clams. Simmer for 15–20 minutes while cooking the noodles in water. When the mushrooms are tender, add the clams and Parmesan. Remove from the heat and serve with the noodles.

"In the way spotted owls are an indicator of the health of an old-growth western hemlock or Douglas fir ecosystem, wilderness is an indicator of the health of the planetary ecosystem. Therefore, wilderness (congressionally designated) needs to be managed in such a way that it retains its wilderness qualities, purity, and health."
—*Rik Smith, Darrington, WA*

Max and Louise
Rik Smith, Glacier Peak Wilderness

MAKES 1 SERVING

1 quart water
2 cups pasta
½ cup onion, chopped
¼–½ pound cheese, cheddar, Monterey Jack, mozzarella, or any combo of the above, grated
½ cup nuts, any variety
Fresh garlic (the more the merrier)
Salt, soy sauce, oregano, basil, chili powder, cumin, cayenne, black pepper, and cinnamon to taste

Prepare the pasta using a minimum of water, so you don't have to pour any out but still have some water covering the noodles. (After a day on the trail, you need the water, and there's all the good pasta juice in it.) The onion, whether fresh or dehydrated, should be added to the water with the pasta. When the pasta is ready, add the cheese, nuts, and garlic. While the cheese is melting, add the spices to taste. The key to this meal, as with all wilderness meals, is to adapt the recipe to the supplies you have in your pack.

Memorable Words on Wilderness

"Wilderness . . . We do not guarantee your enjoyment. We do not guarantee your return!"

—*A homemade sign posted in an area leading to a wilderness in Alaska*

"We have reached the last of our remaining undeveloped lands of this country. I want those remaining lands protected for their natural inherent values now and in the future, for the survival of this country and the world as a whole."
—Gordon Ash, Hungry Horse, MT

Old World Chicken
Gordon Ash, Bob Marshall Wilderness

MAKES 3 TO 4 SERVINGS

1 pound chicken, cut into small pieces
1 teaspoon margarine or vegetable oil
¼ teaspoon curry powder
¼ teaspoon garlic powder
¼ teaspoon sage
¼ teaspoon oregano
¼ teaspoon poultry seasoning
¼ teaspoon onion powder
8-ounce bottle of soy sauce

Put the chicken pieces in a large pan, greased lightly with margarine or vegetable oil. Add the spices and soy sauce. Cook over medium heat until done.

Tips for Desert Camping

- Water means life in the desert; don't be without it! Carry at least 1 gallon of water per person per day in warm weather.

- Heat exhaustion and heat stroke are serious problems. To avoid them, drink lots of water and avoid extreme exertion during the heat of the day.

- Use care when hiking on slickrock (especially if wet). Sandstone is soft and fractures easily. Sand grains can act like ball bearings under your shoes.

- Don't camp in dry streambeds. Flash floods can occur at any time of the year but are most common during the late-summer thunderstorm season.

- Stay on designated trails. Avoid damaging fragile biological soil crust (a dark, crusty covering on the sand) by staying on slickrock when exploring off-trail. An area of mature biological soil crust may take 100 years to develop, but it can be destroyed by just a few steps.

"By crossing the wilderness boundary, I can get away from the stress of the world and enter a land untouched by man, and observe wildlife in its natural habitat. Likewise I want to ensure that this legacy will be around for my four sons. I want them to know that they can go back to the wilderness and see it the same way I did when I was there."

—Ricky E. Brazell, Kamiah, ID

Sheep Herder Potatoes

Ricky E. Brazell, Selway–Bitteroot, Gospel–Hump, and Frank Church–River of No Return Wildernesses

MAKES 2 SERVINGS

1 can whole potatoes
1 can evaporated milk
Salt, pepper, and garlic powder to taste
Flour (optional)

Drain the water off the canned potatoes and dump the potatoes into a pan over medium-high heat. If the pan has been used to cook meat first, you can leave the drippings so they give the potatoes more flavor. With a spatula, start cutting the potatoes as they fry. Once heated, add the can of milk and let it start to simmer. Don't let the pan get too hot or the milk will scorch. Add seasonings to taste. Add flour for thickening if desired.

"Use but don't abuse the wilderness. These truly magnificent areas are a reminder to me of the awesomeness of our Lord who has control of our world."
— Ronald E. Wilcox, Laramie, WY

Fish Chowder
Ronald E. Wilcox, Savage Run Wilderness

MAKES 6 SERVINGS

1 medium onion
6 carrots
6 potatoes
6 celery stalks
Water
6 small trout
10-ounce can corn
Salt and pepper to taste
Fresh garlic to taste (optional)
Pinch of parsley flakes
¼ cup flour
¼ cup powdered milk
Crackers or hot biscuits

Clean and peel the raw vegetables. Chop them into small pieces and add to a pot of boiling water. Cook until tender. In a separate pot, boil the cleaned and beheaded trout for 10 minutes. Remove the trout (save the cooking broth) and let fish cool. Once cool, skin the trout and remove the bones. When vegetables are tender, add the fish, reserved fish broth, can of corn, and seasonings to taste. Combine the flour with powdered milk in a pint jar. Shake well. Add to the vegetable mixture, stirring constantly until the chowder thickens to desired consistency. Serve with crackers or hot biscuits.

"Wilderness is our ancestral home in a neighborhood where there is no doubt that we belong. It is important to go home to remember what we as a species like to forget—that we don't have all the answers."

—*Jonathan W. Klein, Ennis, MT*

Packer's Peppers Magnifique
Jonathan W. Klein, Lee Metcalf Wilderness

MAKES 3 SERVINGS

1 package wheat pilaf (Near East brand preferred)
1 handful raisins
½ cup chopped green onions
Garlic powder to taste
Lemon pepper to taste
2 cups water
1 tablespoon butter or olive oil
3 whole green peppers (gutted)
15 to 18 large slices of favorite cheese

Place the pilaf, raisins, onions, and spices in large pot. Cook the pilaf according to the package directions with water and butter or olive oil. Place the whole green peppers on top of the pilaf mixture while cooking so that they can be steamed soft by the time the pilaf is done (about 25 minutes boiling time). When both pilaf and peppers are done, stuff the peppers with alternating layers of pilaf and cheese until the peppers are bulging. Top with more cheese and eat.

Preserving Archaeological Sites

- If you find Native American artifacts, pictographs, or petroglyphs, show your respect by leaving them alone.

- Don't camp in Native American ruins.

- Save America's past for the future—report damage, theft, and vandalism to the local land managing agency.

"Wilderness is the source material for spiritual and mental liberation."
—John Baas, Walnut Creek, CA

Tortilla Pizza
John Baas, Lake Chelan–Sawtooth Wilderness

MAKES 2 9-INCH PIZZAS

¾ cup water
6-ounce can tomato paste
1 tablespoon dried oregano
1 tablespoon dried basil
1 tablespoon dried thyme
1 tablespoon fresh garlic
1 teaspoon cooking oil
4 9-inch whole wheat tortillas
1 cup pizza toppings of your choice
1 cup grated mozzarella

Combine water with the tomato paste. Add the spices and garlic and stir until the consistency is uniform, adding water to reach the desired thickness of sauce. Heat the sauce to boiling, stirring constantly, then set aside. Make sure your skillet is well oiled. Put 2 tortillas together in the skillet and cook over low heat until brown. Spread half of the sauce on top of one tortilla, add half of the toppings and half of the cheese, cover with the other tortilla and cook for 4 to 5 minutes, or until cheese melts. Repeat with second set of tortillas, and serve.

Memorable Words on Wilderness

"I'm glad I shall never be young without wild country to be young in."
—Aldo Leopold, wilderness leader

"The one thing that I've learned over the years is that it's best to start at the ground floor in working with the public concerning wilderness management. We must work closely with people and not mislead them. The public must have ownership and involvement in the planning process. Only then will our areas be better protected for future generations."

—*Mason C. Miller Jr., Lexington, KY*

Miller's Beef Jerky
Mason C. Miller Jr., Caney Creek Wilderness

24-ounce flank steak
¾ cup red wine
⅓ cup Worcestershire sauce
½ cup soy sauce
1 teaspoon salt or seasoned salt (optional)
1 teaspoon onion powder
½ teaspoon garlic powder
¼ teaspoon pepper (optional)
½ onion, sliced
¾ cup water or more, to dilute taste

To prepare at home: Trim the fat off the steak. Slice the meat against the grain into thin strips. Combine the rest of ingredients. Add the strips of meat, cover tightly, and let sit, refrigerated, overnight. In the morning, drain off the liquid and then arrange meat strips on the oven rack. Put foil below the meat to catch drips. Bake at 150°F for 6 to 8 hours, leaving the oven door slightly open. Turn the oven off and let the jerky sit for about 2 more hours or until dry.

Note: The thickness of the jerky determines the cooking time. Use your own judgment.

Storage: Put the jerky in a plastic bag, close it, and poke several small holes in the bag. Then put the bag into a second bag, and leave the top of the second bag open. Jerky can also be frozen.

DRINKS

"Creation of the National Wilderness Preservation System was the best idea the U.S. ever had. Just think of what we would have lost without it."

—Elizabeth Mejicano, St. George, UT

Non-Black Coffee
Elizabeth Mejicano, Canaan Mountain Wilderness

MAKES 1 SERVING

Coffee (real or instant)
Water
1 to 2 spoonfuls of instant chai

Make 1 cup of coffee. Stir in instant chai to taste. This is a way for those who can't drink coffee black to avoid having to carry in cream or sugar.

Variation: Add hot chocolate mix to taste.

"Wilderness belongs to all of us, not just those who manage the areas or those who live nearby or even those who visit. How devastating to our collective psyches not to have remote, 'pristine' areas set aside to dream about, and to explore in our minds, if not in person."

—Lissa Fahlman, Petersburg, AK

Highbush Cranberry Tea
Lissa Fahlman, Stikine–LeConte Wilderness

MAKES 1 SERVING

1 handful highbush cranberries (picked from the nearest bush)
1 cup water
Dash of honey
Flavored brandy (optional)

Berries can usually be found any time of the year, as a few will last over the winter. Highbush cranberries are best picked after the first frost. Place 8–10 cranberries in a cup. Pour boiling water over the berries and add a taste of honey. Mash the berries to release the flavor. A small amount of brandy can be added as a nightcap. Watch out for seeds.

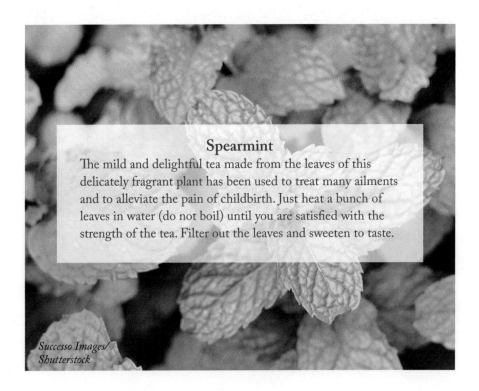

Spearmint
The mild and delightful tea made from the leaves of this delicately fragrant plant has been used to treat many ailments and to alleviate the pain of childbirth. Just heat a bunch of leaves in water (do not boil) until you are satisfied with the strength of the tea. Filter out the leaves and sweeten to taste.

Successo Images/ Shutterstock

"As the world population grows so does the lust for natural silence and space. Having the opportunity to experience the power of wilderness without the intrusion of others is truly the essence of what we seek from wilderness."

—Kari Gunderson, Condon, MT

Paul Toddies
Kari Gunderson, Mission Mountains Wilderness

MAKES 1 SERVING

1 teaspoon Postum or other coffee substitute

1–2 teaspoons hot chocolate mix

1 teaspoon powdered milk

1 dash each cinnamon and vanilla

1 cup water

Mix dry ingredients and vanilla. Boil water. Add water to dry ingredients, stir, and serve.

Variation: Add malted chocolate milk powder (Ovaltine) to taste.

Pine
Pine needles are rich in vitamin C, and they are pleasant to chew on. You can also steep them in boiling water and drink a tea that smells like Christmas.

RYosha/Shutterstock

"I have worked as a seasonal ranger in the backcountry in Rocky Mountain National Park in Colorado since 1980. This traditional drink was developed while I was stationed eight miles in the backcountry sitting by a crackling fire. Bubba's Special will warm your heart and your cold feet."

—*Jim Caretti, Hanceville, AL*

Bubba's Special
Jim Caretti, Rocky Mountain National Park

10 ounces hot water
1 tea bag (green or black tea)
1 packet sweetener (your choice)
1½ ounces Canadian whiskey
Slice of lime

Pour hot water over tea bag in a mug. Add the sweetener, whiskey and a slice of lime. Enjoy.

DESSERT

"I think of wilderness as a place to go to unwind, rest, and restore yourself. After you have left the wilderness, recalling the experience can be calming. I can close my eyes and remember the sounds of loons calling, and see brown bears fishing on Pungokepuk Lake in the Togiak Wilderness, and feel the sun on my face, and hear cactus wrens calling in the Kofa Wilderness."

—Susanna G. Henry, Dillingham, AK

Sandra's Chewy Brownies
Susanna G. Henry, Togiak National Wildlife Refuge

MAKES ABOUT 20 BROWNIES

2 ounces unsweetened baking chocolate
1 cup butter or margarine
1 cup all-purpose flour
1 teaspoon salt
2 cups sugar
1 teaspoon vanilla
1 teaspoon baking powder
3 eggs
½ cup chopped pecans or walnuts (optional)

To prepare at home: Melt the chocolate and butter or margarine on low heat in a large pot, stirring often. Remove from the heat. Add the flour, salt, sugar, vanilla, and baking powder. Mix well. Then add the eggs and mix well again. Add the chopped nuts, if desired. Bake in a greased 9 x 9-inch baking dish in a 350°F oven for 35 minutes. Turn off the oven and allow the brownies to stay in the oven for 10 minutes longer. Remove and cool well before attempting to cut the brownies. These dense brownies pack well, without too much crumbling.

"To me, wilderness means a kind of wild place intricately beautiful beyond understanding."

—Matt Bowser, Kasilof, AK

Cricket Pudding
Matt Bowser, Kenai Wilderness

MAKES 4 SERVINGS

3.4-ounce box of instant pistachio pudding
About 3 tablespoons powdered milk
2 cups water
1 package of Oreo cookies

To prepare at home: Dump the instant pistachio pudding powder and powdered milk into a sealable plastic bag. The bag should be large enough to eventually accommodate the reconstituted pudding and crushed cookies. Remove the white filling from the Oreo cookies and crush the cookies into pea-size crumbles. Pack these in a plastic bag separate from the pudding.

To prepare in the field: Add water to the pudding mix to reconstitute. Knead the contents of the bag to mix the ingredients, then place the pudding in a cold place, such as a mountain stream, a shaded lake, a snowfield, or under some cool moss. Once the pudding has jelled, add the cookies. Serve immediately by squeezing it out of the bag like cake icing.

"Without wilderness we would lose touch with our oneness with nature. Taking care of the wilderness's enduring resources only helps to ensure our species will endure."

—*Penny Roeder, Pagosa Springs, CO*

Chocolate Tortillas
Penny Roeder, South San Juan Wilderness

MAKES 2 SERVINGS

1 tablespoon butter
2 flour tortillas
1 24-ounce chocolate bar

Heat the butter in a skillet. Add 1 tortilla and cook until lightly browned. Flip the tortilla. Add grated or broken-up chocolate according to personal taste. Cover the skillet so the chocolate will melt. Fold the tortilla and enjoy. Repeat.

How Long It Will Last

How long will it last if you leave it behind?

- Paper: 2 to 4 weeks

- Banana peel: 3 to 5 weeks

- Wool cap: 1 year

- Cigarette butt: 2 to 5 years

- Disposable diaper: 10 to 20 years

- Hard plastic container: 20 to 30 years

- Rubber boot sole: 50 to 80 years

- Tin can: 80 to 100 years

- Aluminum can: 200 to 400 years

- Plastic six-pack holder: 450 years

- Glass bottles: Thousands or millions of years

—*Source: Leave No Trace Center for Outdoor Ethics*

"We must manage wilderness with the minimum amount of regulation needed to protect and preserve the resource while allowing wilderness users the greatest amount of personal freedom. Well-trained and well-informed wilderness rangers are the key to accomplishing this job."

—*Frank S. Erickson, Bozeman, MT*

Boy Scout Ice Cream
Frank S. Erickson, Eagle Cap Wilderness

MAKES ENOUGH TO FEED A SMALL TROOP

Fresh snow
1 can sweetened condensed milk (Eagle Brand preferred)
1 can fruit pie filling (cherry and blueberry are my favorites)

Start by placing about 2 quarts of clean snow in a 4-quart or larger bowl. Pour in half of the milk. Mix the snow and milk together with a spoon (a wooden spoon works best) until the mixture has the consistency of ice cream. Adjust the mixture by adding either milk or snow or both as needed. When the mixture is right, pour in the fruit. If things look a little runny, set the entire mixture outside the tent in subzero temperatures. Eat as soon as possible.

Hint: This recipe is best in winter. Summer snow is usually too coarse and dirty to make ice cream.

"Being a wilderness ranger offers the opportunity to apply strong interests in managing resources on the ground and teaching and sharing information with others. It is a great combination of physical work and public interaction in an incredible setting."

—Linda Merigliano, Driggs, ID

Backcountry Cheesecake
Linda Merigliano, Jedediah Smith Wilderness

MAKES 8 SERVINGS

1 tablespoon margarine
1 box no-bake cheesecake mix (Jell-O or Royal brands preferred)
2–4 tablespoons water
⅓ cup powdered milk mixed with 1⅓ cups water
About 1 cup strawberry or blueberry preserves

In the pan you will make the cheesecake in, melt the margarine. Mix in the graham cracker crumbs included in the cheesecake mix. Add just enough water to make stiff paste and press the crust along the bottom of pan. Combine the milk with the filling mix. Pour over the crust. Set in a cool place (a snow bank is great) for about 15 minutes. Voila–instant cheesecake! Garnish with your favorite strawberry or blueberry preserves.

"What I remember most distinctly of my experiences from when I was a wilderness ranger was the sense of serenity that came with being attuned to the earth. I was acutely aware of moon phases, planet orbits, seasonal changes, and wildlife habits. My current excursions into wilderness, though less frequent, still offer the same feeling of wonder and peace through the simple observations of nature in its natural state."

—Rachel (Ondov) Feigley, Livingston, MT

Backcountry Compote
Rachel (Ondov) Feigley, Lee Metcalf Wilderness

MAKES 2 SERVINGS

2–3 cups mixed dried fruit (chop if desired)
4–6 cups water
brown sugar or honey to taste to sweeten
1 pinch cinnamon
Almonds, sunflower seeds, coconut, or trail mix (optional)
Yogurt or whipped cream (a few spoonfuls, as desired)

In a saucepan, barely cover the dried fruit with water. Cook until soft. Add the sweetener, cinnamon, and any optional ingredients (clean out your day pack!). Continue to simmer gently until the liquid forms a syrup. Mix in the yogurt or whipped cream, or dollop on top. Serve on pancakes or alone as dessert.

"The wilderness ranger is a vital link in the education of wilderness users. When more people see the wilderness as a place to cherish and harmonize with, rather than conquer, we will be saving a wilderness that can be enjoyed for generations to come."

—Connie Coulter, Garden Valley, ID

Jell-O Salad
Connie Coulter, Frank Church–River of No Return Wilderness

MAKES 4 SERVINGS

2 cups water
3-ounce package Jell-O mix (any flavor)
Fruit (any kind that will set in gelatin)
½ cup trail mix, candy, or nuts (optional)

Add 1 cup of boiling water, then 1 cup cold water, to the Jell-O. Add fruit and other ingredients as desired. Place in a pan or a container that can be tightly covered. Put the container in a creek for a few hours (or overnight), and the salad will be set and ready to serve.

"Wilderness is where I've met the best friends of my life, and it is a place where my spirit feels truly at home."

—*Margaret Foster, Granby, CO*

Hell Canyon Brownies
Margaret Foster, Indian Peaks Wilderness

¼ cup margarine
1 cup brown sugar
2 eggs
1 cup unbleached flour
½ teaspoon salt
8-ounce package semisweet chocolate chips
6 ounces frozen orange juice
¼ cup coconut
½ cup walnuts
1 teaspoon vanilla

To prepare at home: Cream the margarine, sugar, and eggs. Add all other ingredients. Mix and spread into a shallow, greased 9 x 9-inch pan. Bake at 325°F for 30–35 minutes. Cut into squares and seal in an airtight container to take along on your backcountry trip. These brownies are guaranteed to get you up Hell Canyon and back in a day.

"I see wilderness as a total resource. It is a place of value. The wildlife, the clean air, the natural processes, and the ecosystem are all reasons, in and of themselves, to have designated wilderness areas."

—Gayne Sears, Newport, WA

Pistachio Pudding
Gayne Sears, High Uintas Wilderness

MAKES 4 SERVINGS

3 tablespoons powdered milk (enough to make 2 cups of milk)
2 cups cold water
1 3.4-ounce box of instant pistachio pudding

Mix the powdered milk with water in a 1-quart water bottle. Add the pudding mix. Shake vigorously for 2 minutes. Pour the liquid into cups. Allow to set (the time varies depending on the outside temperature), then serve.

"Listen to the land and to those who know and love that land. Be uncompromising in keeping wilderness free from long-term human impact, for that is the true value of wilderness. Show children the wonder and joy of nearby nature so they may later seek the vastness of wilderness."

—Anne Fege, San Diego, CA

Dried Fruit Crisp

Anne Fege (retired), Forest Service, Washington Office

MAKES 4 SERVINGS

2 cups dried fruit (apples and raisins, or apricots and mixed fruit)
Water, at least 1 cup
½ cup oatmeal
3 tablespoons flour
3 tablespoons sugar
4 tablespoons butter, margarine, or cooking oil
½ cup nuts

Put the fruit in a pot, pour water over the fruit (enough to cover the fruit, at least 1 cup), and soak about 15 minutes until fruit rehydrates. Combine the oatmeal, flour, and sugar in a separate bowl. Grease a frying pan with 1 teaspoon of butter, margarine, or oil, and mix the rest of it into the oatmeal mix. Add nuts to fruit mixture, pour into the pan, and cover with the oatmeal mix. Bake, using a twiggy fire on top of the lid, for about 15 minutes, until the crisp is heated through and browned on the top. Serve warm. If baking at home, top with whipped cream, vanilla ice cream, or yogurt.

(Before savoring the first spoonful, take the time to remember those who patiently taught you outdoor cooking skills. I thank my instructors from three National Outdoor Leadership School expeditions, camp counselors from Girl Scout camps, and my Danish-born mother.)

Memorable Words on Wilderness

"In Wildness is the preservation of the world."
—Henry David Thoreau, philosopher and writer

"I find beauty, peace, adventure, and an acute ability to live in the moment only while being in the wilderness. There is plenty of developed land and not enough undeveloped land; thus the environmental concerns come first."

—Marilyn Krings, Pagosa Springs, CO

Apricot/Peanut Delights
Marilyn Krings, Weminuche Wilderness

    1 package dried apricots
    Water
    1 package rice cakes
    8 ounces peanut butter

Cut the apricots into small pieces. Place in a pan with enough water to barely cover the fruit. Cook slowly until you have a warm, thick paste. Meanwhile, break each rice cake into 4 pieces. Smear with peanut butter. Cover with warm apricot puree and enjoy.

"I love the challenge, beauty, and opportunity wilderness provides for everyone associated with it. I love to teach people how to use the wilderness and still protect and preserve it for future generations."

—*Jim Ficke, Steamboat Springs, CO*

Fruit Squares
Jim Ficke, Flat Tops Wilderness

MAKES 16 TO 20 SQUARES

2 eggs
½ cup honey
⅔ cup flour
1 cup chopped pecans
1 cup chopped fruit (dried apricots, apples, pineapple, pears, raisins)
½ cup chocolate chips (optional)
1 to 2 tablespoons vegetable oil

To prepare at home: Mix the eggs and honey. Add the flour and mix. Blend in the nuts, fruit, and chocolate chips. Scrape into an oiled 8 x 8-inch pan. Bake at 350°F for 30 minutes or until the top begins to brown. Cut into squares and store in an airtight container for your trip.

Wilderness Education

Wilderness Investigations is an educational program and resource for teachers. It offers toolkits and workshops for educators in kindergarten through twelfth grade classrooms. Its materials are place-based, connected to national standards, and can easily be linked to state or district standards or benchmarks. The program is presented by the Arthur Carhart National Wilderness Training Center in Montana.

To learn more, visit educators.wilderness.net

"Maintaining pristine areas to allow future generations a chance to share the beauty with us today is very rewarding. If properly managed, our love for the outdoors will be secured for this generation, as well as many generations to come."
—*Laura Lantz, Duchesne, UT*

High Country Fry Bread
Laura Lantz, High Uintas Wilderness

2 cups flour
1 teaspoon salt
1 tablespoon baking powder
½ tablespoon cooking oil
Water
2 to 3 cups oil (enough to deep-fry the bread)

Mix the dry ingredients. Add ½ tablespoon oil and enough water to make a stiff dough. Knead for 5 minutes. Roll into 3-inch balls and flatten each like a pancake. Cut thin lines from the center to the outside of the pancake (in the shape of a star) so that air can get into the dough. Place the pancake into heated oil in a skillet. Cook until golden brown and crisp.

Variations: Top with refried beans and cheese, veggies and cheese, or honey.

COMPLETE TEXT OF THE WILDERNESS ACT

Public Law 88-577 (16 U.S. C. 1131-1136)

88th Congress, Second Session

September 3, 1964

AN ACT

To establish a National Wilderness Preservation System for the permanent good of the whole people, and for other purposes.

Be it enacted by the Senate and House of Representatives of the United States of America in Congress assembled.

SHORT TITLE

SECTION 1. This Act may be cited as the "Wilderness Act."

WILDERNESS SYSTEM
ESTABLISHED STATEMENT OF POLICY

SECTION 2.(a) In order to assure that an increasing population, accompanied by expanding settlement and growing mechanization, does not occupy and modify all areas within the United States and its possessions, leaving no lands designated for preservation and protection in their natural condition, it is hereby declared to be the policy of the Congress to secure for the American people of present and future generations the benefits of an enduring resource of wilderness. For this purpose there is hereby established a National Wilderness Preservation System to be composed of federally owned areas designated by the Congress as "wilderness areas," and these shall be administered for the use and enjoyment of the American people in such manner as will leave them unimpaired for future use and enjoyment as wilderness, and so as to provide for the protection of these areas, the preservation of their wilderness character, and for the gathering and dissemination of information regarding their use and enjoyment as wilderness; and no Federal lands shall be designated as "wilderness areas" except as provided for in this Act or by a subsequent Act.

(b) The inclusion of an area in the National Wilderness Preservation System notwithstanding, the area shall continue to be managed by the Department and agency having jurisdiction thereover immediately before its inclusion in the National Wilderness Preservation System unless otherwise provided by Act of Congress. No appropriation shall be available for the payment of expenses or salaries for the administration of the National Wilderness Preservation System as a separate unit nor shall any appropriations be available for additional personnel stated as being required solely for the purpose of managing or administering areas solely because they are included within the National Wilderness Preservation System.

DEFINITION OF WILDERNESS

(c) A wilderness, in contrast with those areas where man and his works dominate the landscape, is hereby recognized as an area where the earth and its community of life are untrammeled by man, where man himself is a visitor who does not remain. An area of wilderness is further defined to mean in this Act an area of undeveloped Federal land retaining its primeval character and influence, without permanent improvements or human habitation, which is protected and managed so as to preserve its natural conditions and which (1) generally appears to have been affected primarily by the forces of nature, with the imprint of man's work substantially unnoticeable; (2) has outstanding opportunities for solitude or a primitive and unconfined type of recreation; (3) has at least five thousand acres of land or is of sufficient size as to make practicable its preservation and use in an unimpaired condition; and (4) may also contain ecological, geological, or other features of scientific, educational, scenic, or historical value.

NATIONAL WILDERNESS PRESERVATION SYSTEM— EXTENT OF SYSTEM

SECTION 3.(a) All areas within the national forests classified at least 30 days before September 3, 1964, by the Secretary of Agriculture or the Chief of the Forest Service as "wilderness," "wild," or "canoe" are hereby designated as wilderness areas. The Secretary of Agriculture shall—

(1) Within one year after September 3, 1964, file a map and legal description of each wilderness area with the Interior and Insular Affairs Committees of the United States Senate and the House of Representatives, and such descriptions shall have the same force and effect as if included in this Act: Provided, however, that correction of clerical and typographical errors in such legal descriptions and maps may be made.

(2) Maintain, available to the public, records pertaining to said wilderness areas, including maps and legal descriptions, copies of regulations governing them, copies of public notices of, and reports submitted to Congress regarding pending additions, eliminations, or modifications. Maps, legal descriptions, and regulations pertaining to wilderness areas within their respective jurisdictions also shall be available to the public in the offices of regional foresters, national forest supervisors, and forest rangers.

(b) *(Classification)* The Secretary of Agriculture shall, within ten years after the enactment of this Act, review, as to its suitability or nonsuitability for preservation as wilderness, each area in the national forests classified on September 3, 1964, by the Secretary of Agriculture or the Chief of the Forest Service as "primitive" and report his findings to the President.

(Presidential recommendation to Congress) The President shall advise the United States Senate and House of Representatives of his recommendations with respect to the designation as "wilderness" or other reclassification of each area on which review has been completed, together with maps and a definition of boundaries. Such advice shall be given with respect to not less than one-third of all the areas now classified as "primitive" within three years after the enactment of this Act, and the remaining areas within ten years after the enactment of this Act.

(Congressional approval) Each recommendation of the President for designation as "wilderness" shall become effective only if so provided by an Act of Congress. Areas classified as "primitive" on September 3, 1964, shall continue to be administered under the rules and regulations affecting such areas on September 3, 1964, until Congress has determined otherwise. Any such area may be increased in size by the President at the time he submits his recommendations to the Congress by not more than five thousand acres with no more than one thousand two hundred acres in any one compact unit; if it is proposed to increase the size of any such area by more than five thousand acres or by more than one thousand two hundred and eighty acres in any one compact unit the increase in size shall not become effective until acted upon by Congress. Nothing herein contained shall limit the President in proposing, as part of his recommendations to Congress, the alteration of existing boundaries of primitive areas or recommending the addition of any contiguous area of national forest lands predominantly of wilderness value. Notwithstanding any other provisions of this Act, the Secretary of Agriculture

may complete his review and delete such areas as may be necessary, but not to exceed seven thousand acres, from the southern tip of the Gore Range-Eagles Nest Primitive Area, Colorado, if the Secretary determines that such action is in the public interest.

(c) *(Report to President)* Within ten years after September 3, 1964, the Secretary of the Interior shall review every roadless area of five thousand contiguous acres or more in the national parks, monuments, and other units of the national park system and every such area of, and every roadless island within, the national wildlife refuges and game ranges, under his jurisdiction on September 3, 1964, and shall report to the President his recommendation as to the suitability or nonsuitability of each such area or island for preservation as wilderness.

(Presidential recommendation to Congress) The President shall advise the President of the Senate and the Speaker of the House of Representatives of his recommendation with respect to the designation as wilderness of each such area or island on which review has been completed, together with a map thereof and a definition of its boundaries. Such advice shall be given with respect to not less than one-third of the areas and islands to be reviewed under this subsection within three years after enactment of this Act, not less than two-thirds within seven years of enactment of this Act, and the remainder within ten years of enactment of this Act.

(Congressional approval) A recommendation of the President for designation as wilderness shall become effective only if so provided by an Act of Congress. Nothing contained herein shall, by implication or otherwise, be construed to lessen the present statutory authority of the Secretary of the Interior with respect to the maintenance of roadless areas within units of the national park system.

(d)(1) *(Suitability)* The Secretary of Agriculture and the Secretary of the Interior shall, prior to submitting any recommendations to the President with respect to the suitability of any area for preservation as wilderness—

(A) *(Publication in Federal Register)* give such public notice of the proposed action as they deem appropriate, including publication in the Federal Register and in a newspaper having general circulation in the area or areas in the vicinity of the affected land;

(B) *(Hearings)* hold a public hearing or hearings at a location or locations convenient to the area affected. The hearings shall be announced through such means as the respective Secretaries involved deem appropriate, including notices in the Federal Register and in newspapers of general circulation in the area: Provided; That if the lands involved are located in more than one State, at least one hearing shall be held in each State in which a portion of the land lies;

(C) at least thirty days before the date of a hearing advise the Governor of each State and the governing board of each county, or in Alaska the borough, in which the lands are located, and Federal departments and agencies concerned, and invite such officials and Federal agencies to submit their views on the proposed action at the hearing or by no later than thirty days following the date of the hearing.

(2) Any views submitted to the appropriate Secretary under the provisions of (1) of this subsection with respect to any area shall be included with any recommendations to the President and to Congress with respect to such area.

(e) (Proposed modification) Any modification or adjustment of boundaries of any wilderness area shall be recommended by the appropriate Secretary after public notice of such proposal and public hearing or hearings as provided in subsection (d) of this section. The proposed modification or adjustment shall then be recommended with map and description thereof to the President. The President shall advise the United States Senate and the House of Representatives of his recommendations with respect to such modification or adjustment and such recommendations shall become effective only in the same manner as provided for in subsections (b) and (c) of this section.

USE OF WILDERNESS AREAS

SECTION 4.(a) The purposes of this Act are hereby declared to be within and supplemental to the purposes for which national forests and units of the national park and wildlife refuge systems are established and administered and—

(1) Nothing in this Act shall be deemed to be in interference with the purpose for which national forests are established as set forth in the Act of June 4, 1897 (30 Stat.11), and the Multiple-Use Sustained-Yield Act of June 12, 1960 (74 Stat. 215) (16 U.S.C. 528-531).

(2) Nothing in this Act shall modify the restrictions and provisions of the Shipstead-Nolan Act (Public Law 539, Seventy-first Congress, July 10, 1930; 46 Stat. 1020), the Thye-Blatnik Act (Public Law 733, Eightieth

Congress, June 2, 1948; 62 Stat. 568), and the Humphrey-Thye-Blatnik-Andersen Act (Public Law 607, Eighty-fourth Congress, June 22, 1956; 70 Stat. 326), as applying to the Superior National Forest or the regulations of the Secretary of Agriculture.

(3) Nothing in this Act shall modify the statutory authority under which units of the national park system are created. Further, the designation of any area of any park, monument, or other unit of the national park system as a wilderness area pursuant to this Act shall in no manner lower the standards evolved for the use and preservation of such park, monument, or other unit of the national park system in accordance with the Act of August 25, 1916, the statutory authority under which the area was created, or any other Act of Congress which might pertain to or affect such area, including, but not limited to, the Act of June 8, 1906 (34 Stat. 225; 16 U.S.C. 432 et seq.); section 3(2) of the Federal Power Act (16 U.S.C. 796 (2)); and the Act of August 21, 1935 (49 Stat. 666; 16 U.S.C. 461 et seq.).

(b) Except as otherwise provided in this Act, each agency administering any area designated as wilderness shall be responsible for preserving the wilderness character of the area and shall so administer such area for such other purposes for which it may have been established as also to preserve its wilderness character. Except as otherwise provided in this Act, wilderness areas shall be devoted to the public purposes of recreational, scenic, scientific, educational, conservation, and historical use.

PROHIBITION OF CERTAIN USES

(c) Except as specifically provided for in this Act, and subject to existing private rights, there shall be no commercial enterprise and no permanent road within any wilderness area designated by this Act and except as necessary to meet minimum requirements for the administration of the area for the purpose of this Act (including measures required in emergencies involving the health and safety of persons within the area), there shall be no temporary road, no use of motor vehicles, motorized equipment or motorboats, no landing of aircraft, no other form of mechanical transport, and no structure or installation within any such area.

SPECIAL PROVISIONS

(d) The following special provisions are hereby made:

(1) Within wilderness areas designated by this Act the use of aircraft or motorboats, where these uses have already become established, may be permitted to continue subject to such restrictions as the Secretary of Agriculture deems desirable. In addition, such measures may be taken as may be necessary in the control of fire, insects, and diseases, subject to such conditions as the Secretary deems desirable.

(2) Nothing in this Act shall prevent within national forest wilderness areas any activity, including prospecting, for the purpose of gathering information about mineral or other resources, if such activity is carried on in a manner compatible with the preservation of the wilderness environment. Furthermore, in accordance with such program as the Secretary of the Interior shall develop and conduct in consultation with the Secretary of Agriculture, such areas shall be surveyed on a planned, recurring basis consistent with the concept of wilderness preservation by the Geological Survey and the Bureau of Mines to determine the mineral values, if any, that may be present; and the results of such surveys shall be made available to the public and submitted to the President and Congress.

(3) *(Mineral leases, claims, etc.)* Notwithstanding any other provisions of this Act, until midnight December 31, 1983, the United States mining laws and all laws pertaining to mineral leasing shall, to the same extent as applicable prior to September 3, 1964, extend to those national forest lands designated by this Act as "wilderness areas"; subject, however, to such reasonable regulations governing ingress and egress as may be prescribed by the Secretary of Agriculture consistent with the use of the land for mineral location and development and exploration, drilling, and production, and use of land for transmission lines, waterlines, telephone lines, or facilities necessary in exploring, drilling, production, mining, and processing operations, including where essential the use of mechanized ground or air equipment and restoration as near as practicable of the surface of the land disturbed in performing prospecting, location, and, in oil and gas leasing, discovery work, exploration, drilling, and production, as soon as they have served their purpose. Mining locations lying within the boundaries of said wilderness areas shall be held and used solely for mining or processing operations and uses reasonably incident thereto; and hereafter, subject to valid existing rights, all patents issued under the mining laws of the United States affecting national forest lands designated by this Act as wilderness areas shall convey title to the mineral deposits within the claim, together with the right to cut and use so much of the mature timber therefrom as may be needed in the extraction, removal, and beneficiation of the mineral deposits, if the timber is not otherwise reasonably available, and if the timber is cut under sound principles of forest management as defined by the national forest rules and regulations, but each such patent shall reserve to the United States all title in or to the surface of the lands and products thereof, and no use of the surface of the claim or the resources therefrom not reasonably required for carrying on mining or prospecting shall be allowed except as otherwise expressly provided in this Act: Provided, That, unless hereafter specifically authorized, no patent within wilderness areas designated by this Act shall issue after December 31, 1983, except for the valid claims existing on or before December 31, 1983. Mining claims located after September 3, 1964, within the boundaries of wilderness areas designated by this Act shall create no rights in excess of those rights which may be patented under the provisions of this subsection. Mineral leases, permits, and licenses covering lands within national forest wilderness areas designated by this Act shall contain such reasonable stipulations as may be prescribed by the Secretary of Agriculture for the protection of the wilderness character of the land consistent with the use of the land for the purposes for which they are leased, permitted, or licensed. Subject to valid rights then existing, effective January 1, 1984, the minerals in lands designated by this Act as wilderness areas are withdrawn from all forms of appropriation under the mining laws and from disposition under all laws pertaining to mineral leasing and all amendments thereto.

(4) *(Water resources and grazing)* Within wilderness areas in the national forests designated by this Act, (1) the President may, within a specific area and in accordance with such regulations as he may deem desirable, authorize prospecting for water resources, the establishment and maintenance of reservoirs, water-conservation works, power projects, transmission lines, and other facilities needed in the public interest, including the road construction and maintenance essential to development and use thereof, upon his determination that such use or uses in the specific area will better serve the interests of the United States and the people thereof than will its denial; and (2) the grazing of livestock, where established prior to September 3, 1964, shall be permitted to continue subject to such reasonable regulations as are deemed necessary by the Secretary of Agriculture.

(5) Other provisions of this Act to the contrary notwithstanding, the management of the Boundary Waters Canoe Area, formerly designated as the Superior, Little Indian Sioux, and Caribou Roadless Areas, in the Superior National Forest, Minnesota, shall be in accordance with regulations established by the Secretary of Agriculture in accordance with the general purpose of maintaining, without unnecessary restrictions on other uses,

including that of timber, the primitive character of the area, particularly in the vicinity of lakes, streams, and portages: *Provided,* That nothing in this Act shall preclude the continuance within the area of any already established use of motorboats.

(6) Commercial services may be performed within the wilderness areas designated by this Act to the extent necessary for activities which are proper for realizing the recreational or other wilderness purposes of the areas.

(7) Nothing in this Act shall constitute an express or implied claim or denial on the part of the Federal Government as to exemption from State water laws.

(8) Nothing in this Act shall be construed as affecting the jurisdiction or responsibilities of the several States with respect to wildlife and fish in the national forests.

STATE AND PRIVATE LANDS
WITHIN WILDERNESS AREAS

SECTION 5.(a) In any case where State-owned or privately owned land is completely surrounded by national forest lands within areas designated by this Act as wilderness, such State or private owner shall be given such rights as may be necessary to assure adequate access to such State-owned or privately owned land by such State or private owner and their successors in interest, or the State-owned land or privately owned land shall be exchanged for federally owned land in the same State of approximately equal value under authorities available to the Secretary of Agriculture:
(Transfers, restriction) Provided, however, that the United States shall not transfer to a State or private owner any mineral interests unless the State or private owner relinquishes or causes to be relinquished to the United States the mineral interest in the surrounded land.

(b) In any case where valid mining claims or other valid occupancies are wholly within a designated national forest wilderness area, the Secretary of Agriculture shall, by reasonable regulations consistent with the preservation of the area as wilderness, permit ingress and egress to such surrounded areas by means which have been or are being customarily enjoyed with respect to other such areas similarly situated.

(c) *(Acquisition)* Subject to the appropriation of funds by Congress, the Secretary of Agriculture is authorized to acquire privately owned land within the perimeter of any area designated by this Act as wilderness if (1) the owner concurs in such acquisition or (2) the acquisition is specifically authorized by Congress.

GIFTS, BEQUESTS, AND CONTRIBUTIONS

SECTION 6.(a) The Secretary of Agriculture may accept gifts or bequests of land within wilderness areas designated by this Act for preservation as wilderness. The Secretary of Agriculture may also accept gifts or bequests of land adjacent to wilderness areas designated by this Act for preservation as wilderness if he has given sixty days advance notice thereof to the President of the Senate and the Speaker of the House of Representatives. Land accepted by the Secretary of Agriculture under this section shall become part of the wilderness area involved. Regulations with regard to any such land may be in accordance with such agreements, consistent with the policy of this Act, as are made at the time of such gift, or such conditions, consistent with such policy, as may be included in, and accepted with, such bequest.

(b) The Secretary of Agriculture or the Secretary of the Interior is authorized to accept private contributions and gifts to be used to further the purposes of this Act.

ANNUAL REPORTS

SECTION 7. At the opening of each session of Congress, the Secretaries of Agriculture and Interior shall jointly report to the President for transmission to Congress on the status of the wilderness system including a list and descriptions of the areas in the system, regulations in effect, and other pertinent information, together with any recommendations they may care to make.

Approved September 3, 1964.

Legislative History:

House Reports: No. 1538 accompanying H.R. 9070 (Committee on Interior & Insular Affairs) and No. 1829 (Committee of Conference).

Senate Report: No. 109 (Committee on Interior & Insular Affairs).

Congressional Record: Vol. 109 (1963):

- April 4, 8, considered in Senate.
- April 9, considered and passed Senate.
- Vol. 110 (1964): July 28, considered in House.
- July 30, considered and passed House, amended, in lieu of H.R. 9070.
- August 20, House and Senate agreed to conference report.

Note: Italicized words in parentheses are editorial additions inserted for clarification.

Get Involved . . .

Become a Wilderness Volunteer

Volunteer to assist in maintaining trails, monitoring impacts, rehabilitating campsites, picking up litter, educating visitors about Leave No Trace techniques, and much more. To make a difference in your area, contact your nearest public lands agency.

SUGGESTED READINGS

To learn more about backcountry cookery, wilderness, and management of designated wilderness, the following books are suggested:

Brinkley, Douglas. *The Wilderness Warrior: Theodore Roosevelt and the Crusade for America*. New York: HarperCollins Publishers, 2009.

Cole, David N., and Laurie Yung, eds. *Beyond Naturalness: Rethinking Park and Wilderness Stewardship in an Era of Rapid Change*. Washington, DC: Island Press, 2010.

Cordell, Ken H., author and ed.; John C. Bergstrom and J. M. Bowker, eds. *The Multiple Values of Wilderness*. State College, PA: Venture Publishing Inc., 2005.

Dawson, Chad P., and John C. Hendee. *Wilderness Management: Stewardship and Protection of Resources and Values*, 4th ed. Golden, CO: Fulcrum Publishing, 2008.

Harvey, Mark. *Wilderness Forever: Howard Zahniser and the Path to the Wilderness Act*. Seattle: University of Washington Press, 2005.

Leopold, Aldo. *A Sand County Almanac and Sketches Here and There*. Oxford University Press, 1949.

Nash, Roderick Frazier. *Wilderness and the American Mind*, 5th ed. New Haven, CT: Yale University Press, 2014.

Pearson, Claudia, ed. *NOLS Cookery*, 6th ed. National Outdoor Leadership School, 2012.

Scott, Doug. *Our Wilderness: America's Common Ground*. Golden, CO: Fulcrum Publishing, 2009.

———. *The Enduring Wilderness: Protecting Our Natural Heritage through the Wilderness Act*. Golden, CO: Fulcrum Publishing, 2004.

Turner, James Morton. *The Promise of Wilderness: American Environmental Politics since 1964*. Seattle: University of Washington Press, 2012.

Wilderness Explorer: Jr. Ranger Activities and Adventures for All Ages. Wilderness Educators, 2014. Download at educators.wilderness.net.

Zahniser, Howard. *The Wilderness Writings of Howard Zahniser*. Mark Harvey, ed. Seattle: University of Washington Press, 2014.

To learn more, visit these websites:

Bureau of Land Management Wilderness
blm.gov/wo/st/en/prog/blm_special_areas/NLCS/Wilderness.html

Forest Service Wilderness
fs.fed.us/recreation/programs/cda/wilderness.shtml

National Park Service Wilderness
wilderness.nps.gov

U.S. Fish and Wildlife Service National Wildlife Refuge System
www.fws.gov/refuges/whm/wilderness.html

Celebrating 50 Years of American Wilderness
wilderness50th.org (site available through 2015)

Wilderness.net
www.wilderness.net

Society for Wilderness Stewardship
wildernessstewardship.org

Arthur Carhart National Wilderness Training Center
carhart.wilderness.net

Aldo Leopold Wilderness Research Institute
leopold.wilderness.net

National Wilderness Stewardship Alliance
wildernessalliance.org

INDEX